Does Monogamy Work?

The Big Idea   Luke Brunning

Does Monogamy Work?

A primer for the 21st century

Over 160 illustrations

General Editor:
Matthew Taylor

Contents

Introduction

A

Does monogamy work?

Doubtless we have asked this question of our own relationships or of those of people we know. On the one hand, the ideal of monogamy promises love, intimacy and lifelong companionship. On the other, monogamy requires us to forego all other sex and romance. For some, this is an easy choice; for others, a cause of ambivalence. In this book, we take this ambivalence seriously by exploring monogamy's origins, the contemporary pressures experienced by monogamous people and some responses to those pressures, including the adoption of nonmonogamy.

The **golden age of marriage** occurred in western cultures during the 1950s and 1960s. This was the heyday of marriage and the nuclear family, when fathers provided the main income, and mothers stayed at home. Despite the widespread myth, this form of apparently 'traditional' marriage has been rare throughout history.

The UK **Divorce Reform Act** of 1969 introduced new legislation that meant spouses no longer had to evidence significant fault in order to end a marriage, 'irretrievable breakdown' became sufficient. William Wilson (1913–2010), the MP who introduced the legislation, noted that 'though marriages are made in heaven, they don't always stay there'.

Although we may wish it were otherwise, monogamy is a contingent form of romantic life rather than an evidently 'natural' way to love and raise families. Monogamy is predominantly a social ideal, so it is vulnerable to social change. We will learn, for example, what Roman slavery, social inequality and early Christianity have to do with monogamy, and how the monogamy ideal was shaped by successive social upheavals, from industrialization to inflation, farming to feminism.

Monogamous wedlock has been under siege since the 'golden age of marriage' in the 1950s, with rising divorce rates, increasing cohabitation, sexual liberation and new visions of romantic life. In Britain, for example, divorce rates rapidly increased in the 1970s after the introduction of the Divorce Reform Act of 1969. They peaked in the 1990s, with around 14 divorces per 1,000 marriages. Since then, rates of divorce have fallen slightly, but only because the overall marriage rate has plummeted, dropping by 50% between the 1960s and 1970s alone. According to the Office for National Statistics in the UK, in 2016, 243,000 opposite-sex couples married, compared to 471,000 in 1940; 88% of couples were cohabiting before marriage; only 24% of marriages were religious and the average age of men getting married for the first time was 37.9 years and for women 35.5 years. By 2018, the average length of a marriage that ended in divorce was a mere 12.5 years.

A For many people, monogamous marriage is the ideal form of relationship; the ultimate expression of love and commitment, and the best context in which to raise a family.

B A woman cuts into the cake at her 'divorce party'. Today many couples divorce out a diffuse sense that they are no long compatible, or that their desires pull in different directions: evidence of how marital ideals have changed dramatically in recent decades.

B

Responses to these facts could include making greater efforts to make a marriage work, modifying our expectations of monogamy or exploring other options, such as open relationships or polyamory. Could changing marriage institutions so that monogamous couples are not privileged actually make it easier to be monogamous? Might adopting polyamory enable people to flourish romantically, and raise families, without conflict and jealousy?

Strictly speaking 'monogamy' denotes 'marriage' to one person. The opposite of monogamy is polygamy, marriage to multiple people. Talk of polygamy conjures images of one man with multiple wives, but that is properly termed polygyny, and the practice of a woman having multiple husbands is called polyandry.

A

A   Despite media attention focusing on white, affluent liberals, polyamorous relationships are incredibly diverse, and encompass differences in gender, sex, sexual orientation, political views and religion.

B   De Beauvoir viewed her non-exclusive relationship with Sartre as her greatest achievement. Their personal life was reflective of their philosophical explorations of freedom.

B

Polyamory means 'many loves', and is is a neologism which blends Greek (*poly-*) and Latin (*amor*) to describe people who can romantically love several people at once.

Polygamy, or plural marriage, is has been widely practised historically. Today it is mostly found in Africa and Asia.

Polygyny is where one man marries several women, and is what most people imagine when they think of plural marriage. The term is also used to describe non-human animals who mate with several females.

Polyandry is a form of plural marriage where one woman marries several men. Polyandry is typically found in hunter-gatherer or agricultural societies, and is most prevalent in the Plateau of Tibet, a region straddling India, China and Tibet.

In this book, use of the term 'monogamy' covers any romantic relationship that is dyadic (between two people) and exclusive (does not involve any other people). Dyadicity and exclusivity can come apart. The group marriage of Draupadi to the five sons of King Pandu, as described in the ancient Hindu epic *Mahābhārata*, might be described as exclusive, in that none of them were intimate with people outside their group, whereas the dyadic marriage between the philosophers Jean-Paul Sartre (1905–80) and Simone de Beauvoir (1908–86) was a nonexclusive open relationship. In this book, unless specified, 'monogamous' and 'nonmonogamous' will not refer to marital unions only.

A

Monogamy is a social practice in which behaviour is evaluated against norms and ideals that prescribe what our romantic relationships, and their place in our lives, should look like. The three central dimensions of the monogamy ideal concern love, sex and character. If we are monogamous, we are understood to be monoamorous, in that we only love one person romantically. We are also understood to be monosexual, in that we only have sex with one person. Finally, we are understood to be partisan, in that we are romantically closed to other people.

Other facets of the monogamy ideal include the notion that we ought to have a domestic life with a romantic partner, share goals and values, disclose information and do many activities together.

B

People commonly think monogamous relationships should deepen over time, becoming more serious and committed as two lives entwine. This progression is sometimes called the 'relationship escalator', because monogamous relationships are held to move from courtship towards commitment, marriage and the creation of a family. Like an escalator, the ideal monogamous relationship has a clear direction of travel; we cannot move easily in the opposite direction.

In her article 'Monogamy's Law' (2004), legal scholar
Elizabeth Emens describes 'supermonogamy': an extreme
version of the monogamy ideal where people think there
is just one person for them and seek a relationship with
'the one' or 'Mr Right'. This idea is entwined with the norm
that Elizabeth Brake, in her book *Minimizing Marriage*
(2012), calls 'amatonormativity': the claim that all humans
want a single amorous relationship, and that amorous
relationships should be preferred to other kinds of
relationship, such as friendship.

People disagree about monogamy's
practical implications. Must
people be monogamous to raise
children? Should a monogamous
couple always live together? Is
their relationship deficient if they
lack shared activities, or are often
apart? Is it wrong to flirt with a
colleague, share bad news with
friends before a partner, go on
holiday with a close friend of a
different gender, not tell a current
partner about an ex?

Can a partner be attracted to other people as long as they do not act on it, or should they not feel attraction in the first place? And so on.

These are disputes about what is central to monogamy, not disputes about the value of monogamy. Perhaps the most crucial of these differences of opinion concerns emotional and sexual exclusivity. Some monogamous people value emotional exclusivity over sexual exclusivity, viewing 'emotional' affairs as more of a threat to their relationship than sexual affairs; others might be happy their partner has intimate emotional bonds with others as long as they remain sexually exclusive. Sexual exclusivity is often thought to be the most 'natural' aspect of monogamy, a consequence of our biological nature. Chapter 1 examines the origins of monogamy, and considers how 'natural' it really is to humans.

B

1. The Origins of Monogamy

A

Today, monogamy is the dominant relationship form. Most people across the world either have, or aspire to have, a monogamous partner. This is so despite global variation in how families are structured, marriages contracted and sexuality enacted. Despite disagreement about the precise requirements of monogamy, people are united in viewing it positively. In one study, for example, psychologist Terri Conley and colleagues found that their interviewees typically mentioned eight specific benefits that monogamous relationships bring:

a sense of commitment, trust, moral propriety, feelings of meaning, passion, sex, health and family. The same interviewees thought nonmonogamous relationships performed worse along each dimension.

Egalitarianism is the idea that all humans are equal. Different kinds of egalitarians draw different normative conclusions from the idea that people have equal moral status. Some think social conditions should be equalized (e.g. equal rights, wealth and resources), whereas others focus instead on equalizing opportunities.

Monogamy has been attributed a range of other benefits. In a review article of the human sciences, 'The Puzzle of Monogamous Marriage' (2012), Joseph Henrich and colleagues argue that cultural evolutionary pressures favoured monogamy due to group benefits. By reducing the numbers of unpartnered men, monogamy supposedly helped reduce crime, and by lessening competition decreased gender inequality. They also speculate that the rise of monogamy 'may have helped create the conditions for the emergence of democracy and political equality at all levels of government', because monogamous relationships involve a basic form of egalitarianism.

A   Modern individualism can make it hard to notice that worldwide the history of marriage is predominantly one of groups coming together. By uniting families, and securing property for future generations, marriages helped stabilize societies. These functions were vital because most marriages were between people living mere miles from each other. Today, marriage has been transformed by industrialization, globalization and the movement of people.

Henrich and his colleagues also argue that monogamy benefits families and children. In a monogamous society men do not seek additional wives, thus retaining more time and money for childcare and the household. Similarly, they note that most people in monogamous families are closely related, unlike in polygamous families where children often have different parents. Proximity to non- or distant relations is correlated strongly with instances of child abuse, neglect and family conflict.

A Some cultures have instituted complex forms of imperial nonmonogamy. Cixi (1835–1908), a low-ranking wife of the Xianfeng Emperor (1831–61), scaled the formal hierarchy of Qing Dynasty concubines after providing the emperor with an heir, to eventually seize power herself.

B Today, polygamy is distributed unevenly across the globe. Although formally banned in some places, the practice is often still tolerated, particularly amongst social elites who are more adept at avoiding censure.

A

Because of its sway and its seeming benefits, monogamy can seem *universal* and *natural*. But the truth is murkier.

From a broader historical and cultural perspective monogamy's recipe looks more complex: part genetic stratagem, part capacity to love, part obliging context. Long before monogamy triumphed as an ethically captivating 'idea', people embraced it in response to their social situation.

Societies where monogamy is the only acceptable relationship type are outliers. In studying the Human Relations Area Files, historian Walter Scheidel suggests that between 76 and 77% of distinct global cultures, both historically and now (for which we have sufficient evidence), practise some form of polygyny, and only between 17 and 21% of these cultures are exclusively monogamous. The percentage of cultures that condone other forms of nonmonogamy, such as concubinage, is arguably higher.

The **Human Relations Area Files** at Yale University, USA, is a resource developed since the 1930s to help anthropologists document and understand different human cultures around the world, both as they exist now and historically.

Concubinage has historically meant a person (a concubine), usually a woman, living with a man out of wedlock. Concubinage was usually an established social status inferior to that of recognized wives, but this varied with context.

Not everyone in polygynous societies was nonmonogamous; polygyny is often for elites only. Social scientists Charles Welch and Paul Glick, in their article 'The Incidence of Polygamy in Contemporary Africa: A Research Note' (1981), report that only around 25% of all marriages in the 14 African countries studied were polygamous (e.g. 27.3% in Gabon, 26.2% and 27.1% in Tanzania).

Data on current polygynous societies is similar. The United Nations Population Division's report on marriage, for example, which was based on data conducted between 2000 and 2010, states that 'in 26 out of the 35 countries with data on polygamy, between 10 per cent and 53 per cent of women aged 15–49 had co-wives'. These countries range from Algeria to Kenya and the UAE. The difference in incidence of polygamy depends on many factors: the culture, whether polygamy is legal, the availability of partners and so on.

B

THE LEGAL STATUS OF POLYGAMY AROUND THE WORLD

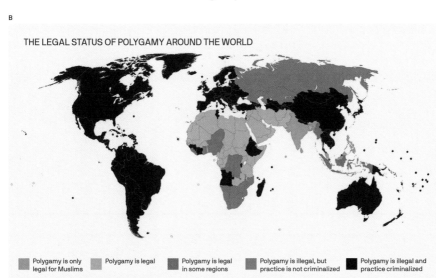

Polygamy is only legal for Muslims   Polygamy is legal   Polygamy is legal in some regions   Polygamy is illegal, but practice is not criminalized   Polygamy is illegal and practice criminalized

Imperialism means to extend one country's power and influence through the colonization of other countries. For instance the Roman Emperor Trajan (d. AD 117) ruled over many distinct territories, from North Africa to Northern England; Spain to Babylonia. Imperial rule relied on military expansion and control, extractive taxation and the ability to expropriate labour and resources.

Fundamentalist Mormonism is a 19th-century variant of Christianity founded by Joseph Smith (1805–44), who introduced the Book of Mormon, which describes God's relationship with the Americas. Fundamentalist Mormons retain original practices which have been discarded by mainstream Mormons, such as polygyny and collectivism.

Plural marriages, both now and historically, often reflect social status. To take an extreme historical example, in *c.* 1615 the Quechua Peruvian nobleman Felipe Guáman Poma de Ayala (*c.* 1535–*c.* 1615) described the Inca ordinance in which the size of polygynous unions mirrored political and institutional structures: 'We order that the *caciques* (high officials), have fifty women for their service and for their increase in population in this kingdom; *huno curaca* (chief of ten thousand), thirty women; *uamanin apo* (regional lord), twenty women... A poor Indian would have two women.'

This window into Inca society starkly reveals the relationship between resources, population and power, and hints at tangled connections between imperialism and monogamy. Such vast disparities between men and women could only be the result of conquest.

A

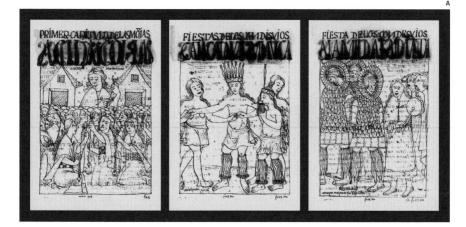

B

A   Illustrations from Felipe
    Guáman Poma de Ayala's
    17th-century text on Inca
    customs.
B   A 19th-century Mormon
    family. Large biological
    families were spiritually
    significant to early
    Mormons, and polygyny
    is still practised by some
    Mormon fundamentalists.

Similar stratification exists within many polygynous societies today, albeit often unofficially. Among the Dinka of South Sudan, for example, men with the economic advantage of large herds of cattle can access more wives and thus the prestige associated with larger families. In such societies, monogamous unions are symbols of social disadvantage.

In case these societies seem exceptional, we should note the contemporary breadth of nonmonogamy. Today, nonmonogamy exists on every inhabited continent. Polygamy is legally recognized in many countries in Africa and the Middle East, and is permitted for Muslims in other states, too, such as India and Singapore. In 2011, the United Nations research suggested that polygamy was legal or widely accepted in 33 countries, and legal for parts of the population in 41 countries. Polygamy is practised illegally in other places, for example among some fundamentalist Mormon communities in North America, where polygamy was only prohibited after the Reynolds v. United States ruling of 1879.

A Someone who practises fraternal polyandry, such as the Tibetan woman here, is married to two or more brothers. The practice can be a response to scarce resources, as it prevents family land being divided when each brother marries.

B A Tibetan woman and her three husbands, all brothers. In some cultures, fraternal polyandry has been associated with the idea of shared paternity, where one child is thought to be the offspring, and thus the social responsibility, of several men.

C William Blake's illustrations of *The Creation of Eve* and *Satan Watching the Caresses of Adam and Eve*, taken from John Milton's *Paradise Lost* (1808). The prized status of monogamy is visible in mythical origin stories. Although, as with the biblical story, these often entrench other norms too, such as patriarchy.

The true reach of nonmonogamy becomes clear when we focus on its rarest form: polyandry, where women marry several men.

Polyandry has been thought of as extremely rare and confined to the Tibetan Plateau. But a re-evaluation of the ethnographical record by anthropologists Katherine Starkweather and Raymond Hames in 2012 showed that even polyandry has a global reach, emerging in some form in 53 societies, including the !Kung in southern Africa, some Mongolian societies in Asia, the Dieri in Australia, the Aleut in North America, the Yanomamö of South America and the Sakai of Southeast Asia.

Despite such cultural variety, in terms of sheer population the world is clearly monogamous, and most societies that historically permitted some from of polygyny, like China, have now adopted monogamy. What accounts for this change? What are the origins of monogamy?

Origin stories depend, in part, on a conception of our original state. Is polygyny's historical prevalence an aberration, from which we are now recovering, or is the move to monogamy a step away from an originally promiscuous state?

Answers to this question have their own history. The biblical creation story, as outlined in Genesis, appears to suggest the original state of mankind was monogamous. Genesis 2:24 in the King James Bible, reads: 'Therefore [after the creation of woman] shall a man leave his father and his mother, and shall cleave unto his wife: and they shall be one flesh.' This verse offers a popular vision of the original monogamous union. From this religious perspective, subsequent polygyny deviates from this ideal.

c

A

Others inverted the biblical story to view monogamy not as our original state, but as the fruit of a civilizing process. For the Enlightenment philosopher Jean-Jacques Rousseau, writing in his *Discourse on the Origin and Foundations of Inequality Among Men* (1755) – more than a century before the theories of Charles Darwin – the primitive condition of 'nascent man' was such that 'one particular craving goaded him to perpetuate his own species: and this blind inclination, devoid of any sentiment of the heart, occasioned only a purely animal act. Once the need was satisfied, the two sexes no longer recognized each other, and even the child meant nothing to the mother once he could do without her.' This vision of a primitive state awash with brief animalistic sex, devoid of sustained relationships and free from inequality was a far cry from the enduring union of one flesh portrayed in the Bible.

B

C

Jean-Jacques Rousseau (1712–78) was a Geneva-born philosopher and novelist. He is best known for his ethical, political and moral-psychological writings.

Charles Darwin (1809–82) is synonymous with the theory of evolution as natural selection which explains how species are formed as a result of changes to inheritable characteristics that help individuals survive in their environment.

Nascent man means the earliest form of man. Jean-Jacques Rousseau suggests that self-regard (amour propre) played a pivotal role in the move away from the egalitarian, yet 'primitive' societies of nascent people.

Friedrich Engels (1820–95) was a businessman in the cotton industry who later became a revolutionary leader and popularizer of the thinking of Karl Marx.

For Rousseau, the 'first revolution' of such a society into a more 'civilized' one – with rudimentary systems of property, domestic life and the sexual division of labour – was a positive change. The fruit of the civilizing process, although prone to spoiling, was fundamentally sweet.

Others adopted a more negative stance. Two decades after the publication of Darwin's *On the Origins of Species by Means of Natural Selection* (1859), Friedrich Engels developed some ideas of Karl Marx (1818–83) into an account of the origin of the monogamous family called *The Origin of the Family, Private Property and the State* (1884). He describes an original state of group marriage, free of distinctions and a sense of ownership. His state of nature was more caring and less carnal than Rousseau's, and not to be viewed through 'brothel spectacles'.

Yet for Engles, the victory of private property over common ownership, and the need for clear inheritance, was to blame for monogamy's eventual ascendancy. For him, the fruit of the civilizing process was fundamentally bitter; monogamy's contemporary dominance is a fall from grace.

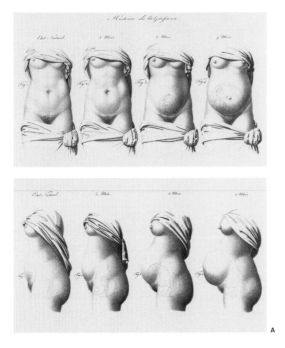

A **pair-bond** is a persisting close attachment between two mating animals. A significant majority of birds form lasting pair-bonds to raise chicks together and some, like cranes, mate together for life.

Serial monogamy means having several emotionally and sexually exclusive relationships over a lifetime which do not overlap. The term is often used to describe people who lurch from short relationship to short relationship.

A

Today's 'state of nature' stories of human development are informed by evolutionary biology. Human behaviour is understood in terms of what best serves the interests of our genes, and those of our close kin (with whom we share many identical genes) given (1) the constraints of our biological nature and (2) our environment.

From this perspective, it might be thought we are clearly evolved to be monogamous. After all, humans have a long gestation period during which the mother is vulnerable, and long post-partum periods when infants are helpless. If infants are to survive (and genes inherited), they and their mothers require extensive support. A good mechanism for providing this support is the pair-bond, in which both parents have a relationship and care for the infant together.

Although uplifting, this story is an inaccurate explanation of monogamy's dominance. Less than 3% of mammals in the animal kingdom are reported to be monogamous (exceptions include some species of shrew, bat, possum and marmoset), and there is no clear scientific consensus that our biological make-up inclines humans towards monogamy. From a gene's perspective, all that matters is survival in offspring, so support could be provided by other individuals, such as our relatives or community. Indeed, these arrangements are very common. In the modern world, where it is usual for two parents to work, for example, grandparents and extended family play an important role in raising children. British sit-com *Raised by Wolves* (2013–16) centres on single mother Della bringing up her six children with the aid of her father, and in Northern Irish sit-com *Derry Girls* (2018–) protagonist Erin lives with her aunt, cousin and grandfather as well as her parents, illustrating the array of alternative family structures available, besides the traditional 'nuclear family' arrangement.

Moreover, one individual could conceivably have several pair-bonds at the same time, just as individuals may have several kinship bonds at once.

Even if pair bonding is incompatible with polygyny, any evolutionary link between pair-bonds and monogamy would fall short of the contemporary monogamy ideal, in which relationships are ideally permanent. From the genetic perspective, things are as Rousseau envisaged: once offspring are independent, parents can look elsewhere for new partners, in other words embrace serial monogamy.

A   A 19th-century illustration of the stages of pregnancy. Monogamy has often been viewed through a biological, and specifically evolutionary, lens. The historicity of this view is not a reason to value it, however.

B   Emphasis on the pair-bond may cause us to overlook other kinds of familial and communal care. In many societies, children are raised by several individuals or within large families.

At the heart of all reproductive behaviour lies a tension between offspring quantity and offspring quality. Individuals must balance the need to care for existing offspring against additional reproductive opportunities. The costs of the latter are often low for males, whose reproductive strategies reflect the fact they have abundant gametes.

Depending on the specific context, then, serial monogamy, polygyny or monogamy with extracurricular sex, when easy to perform, may help strike the balance between maintaining offspring quality and quantity.

We often change our context, too, by manipulating our environment or developing new practices and instructions, thereby altering the field on which our biologically constrained dependency plays out. The amount of alienable resources – food, livestock, clothing, weapons etc – is crucial in shaping relationships in a society. Resources help us care for our offspring and, perhaps more importantly, to attract mates. Practically speaking, however, resources are scarce, and scarcity sparks competition. Attention to this fact helps us understand why monogamy arose first as a marital institution and then, only later, once the social practice had sufficient momentum, as a sexual ideal.

A

A   A 15th-century marriage chest. Marriage has not only served as a way of preserving or transferring resources, but also as an occasion to display wealth, too, whether through expensive gifts, parties or dresses.
B   Dynastic marriages shaped more than just family politics. The marriage of Ferdinand of Aragon and Isabella of Castile, shown here worshipping the Virgin Mary, in a panel painted c. 1497 by Fray Pedro de Salamanca, produced a single religious polity with vast global implications.

Gametes are reproductive cells. In humans, sperm and eggs are gamete cells. They fuse together to form the zygote, which develops into an embryo.

Dynastic marriages united two significant families for mutual benefit. These unions would be carefully negotiated by the families (and governments) concerned, and were aimed at consolidating political power. Queen Elizabeth I (1533–1603) frustrated her advisors through her inability to settle on a marriage candidate.

B

Marriage is an institution for accumulating, preserving and transferring resources among cooperative groups.

'Resource' must be understood broadly to include wealth, but also labour, care and forms of knowledge. As family historian Stephanie Coontz notes in *Marriage, a History* (2005): 'Probably the single most important function of marriage throughout most of history, although it is almost completely eclipsed today, was its role in establishing cooperative relationships between families and communities.'

In the Middle Ages, marriage helped couples establish businesses, with each spouse contributing tools, capital or expertise to the union. Today, the support of two families may enable a couple to put a deposit on a house, or benefit from childcare. Dynastic marriages offer the ultimate example of pooled resources. The very existence of Spain as a distinct nation state, for example, originated in the marriage between Isabella I (1451–1504) and Ferdinand II (1452–1516) in 1469 and the melding of their respective territories of Castile and Aragon.

A Wars can dramatically change the sex ratio of a society. Here, the German Emperor Wilhelm II (1859–1941) is depicted being tormented by women grieving for sons and lovers lost in the Second World War.

B The loss of a wife or child could have a devastating impact on small farms and their communities. Larger families were more resilient in the face of tragedy.

Monogamous marriage only emerged as a stable practice when social conditions made it both desirable and practicable for many people. Since conditions vary globally, monogamy likely had many separate origins. Underpinning its rise is the complex interplay of resource, stability and equality.

A society's sex ratio is the first factor to consider. Because significant inequalities in the numbers of men and women generate pressures away from monogamy, more equitable ratios may support monogamy. Disease, war and patterns of labour migration may destabilize the balance of sexes within a group. Traditionally, war and mobile labour were the preserve of men. If there are fewer men in a society, polygyny might be the only option available to many women who want to marry.

Additionally, we must consider a society's basic economic structure. How are its resources generated? A potted history of change would start with nomadic foraging groups. Their societies are small, mobile, with few alienable resources. They are vulnerable to hostile environments, so cooperation outweighs competition. Even if relationships were 'monogamous' and individuals developed a sexual and caring bond with one person, the communal perspective, not the nuclear unit, would structure the accumulation, distribution and transfer of resources, and the care of children. Since the communal perspective dominates, no social institution of marriage is required.

Now consider agricultural societies. Farms enable some people to accumulate and store resources, but only if they command an ample workforce with ties to the land. Family is a good source of this dependable labour if your fertility rate is high. Perhaps initially, then, the promise and power of agricultural innovation favoured polygyny. The wealth of male farmers enabled them to afford additional wives; additional wives meant more offspring to work the land, which, in turn, meant more wealth.

B

Labour migration happens when people move between countries, or within their country of origin, to seek work. Migrants contribute greatly to the countries in which they work, and often also send money home.

A   Elizabeth Hardwick (1527–1608) acquired substantial wealth and social status in Elizabethan England through four shrewd marriages. Here she is depicted (left) by Hans Eworth

c. 1560s when married to Sir William Cavenish and (right) by Rowland Lockey in 1592 when married to her fourth husband, George Talbot, 6th Earl of Shrewsbury.

B   Industrialization had a rapid impact on the family. Factories could employ parents and children, and provide stable wages throughout the year, but industrial life was inflexible.

As societies grew, however, and hierarchies were established, rulers and elites accrued vastly unequal holdings of land, resources and marital and sexual partners. Scheidel reports: 'Under the Western Zhou dynasty in ancient China, the emperor had access to one queen, three consorts, nine wives of second rank, twenty-seven wives of third rank, and eighty-one concubines.' Lowly officials also benefited.

Inequalities of power, wealth and partners risked creating social instability as it became harder for men to find wives, have children, maintain labour-intensive farms and preserve property. Laura Betzig argues that marital monogamy was instigated by despotic leaders, as a compromise with citizens: you can have access to wives *if* you support my rule.

Irrespective of whether such compromises were made, or lasted, Satoshi Kanazawa and Mary Still make the important point that the independent choice of a large number of women to marry monogamously rather than polygynously also contributed to this shift.

Women and their families can lose much through poor marital choices, so they will only marry monogamously when it is advantageous to do so. War, revolution, political change and the entrenchment of an engaged patrician elite reduced social stratification in despotic agrarian societies. As a result, as more men acquired land and resources, individual women and their families would be more inclined to favour monogamy. Thus monogamy emerged as an attractive option for ordinary people as a way of navigating the increasingly complex ties between land, wealth and family.

Finally, consider industrialization. As industry replaces agriculture as the main source of a society's wealth, people start exchanging labour for wages. In wage societies, high fertility can be burdensome: more mouths, fewer wages. Smaller families, or those less tied to land, can also react better to the demands of the industrial economy: moving from countryside to city, and from factory to factory. The ideology of industry, which offers the reward of social mobility in return for hard work and personal achievement, also resonates better with monogamous families.

B

Monogamy helped streamline matters of paternity and inheritance.

A For centuries, royal legitimacy was necessary for social and political stability. This vast painting by Lucas de Heere (1534–84), commissioned by Queen Elizabeth I, depicts her as the culmination of the Tudor line, and therefore the legitimate ruler.

B Many sex workers in the Ancient world, like the women depicted in this fresco from Pompei, were slaves. Slavery enabled men to exploit women sexually whilst preserving the morally distinct institution of marriage.

In the domestic context, evident paternity and smaller family groups aided the transfer and preservation of resources through the generations. In the political context, monogamous marriage (although not sexual monogamy) helped produce identifiable heirs, vital for social stability if power and land ownership were hereditary. The absence of an heir often generated conflict. England was plunged into turmoil and war when Edward the Confessor (c. 1003–66) died with no heir, and Henry VIII's (1491–1547) need for an heir to preserve the Tudor line led to two executed wives and contributed to the European Reformation.

A

B

The **European Reformation** burst into life in 1517 when Martin Luther (1483–1546) publicly challenged the Catholic Church's efforts to raise money in exchange for a reduced stint in purgatory. The ensuing emergence of various Protestant confessions, including the Church of England, initiated a series of monumental intellectual, social and political changes.

The social institution of slavery, in the context of imperialism, played an interesting role in the emergence of monogamy. Ancient Greece and Rome, two quintessential slaving societies, were anomalous in legally mandating monogamous marriage. Why? Slavery enabled monogamous marriage to be supplemented by the socially condoned sexual exploitation of slaves. Wealthy citizens could therefore strike the balance between building good families and estates, *and* maximizing their reproductive potential, without having to marry polygynously and appropriate female citizens to the detriment of other male citizens.

Imperial appropriation also enabled elites to accrue wealth without creating domestic shortages for citizens. Also, slave labour gave many in society the time and social 'space' to become engaged, invested and educated citizens. These social conditions proved instrumental for the emergence of democracy, but they also fostered an egalitarian ideal of monogamous marriage, at least among the social elite.

A   A 6th-century wedding ring depicting eight scenes from the life of Christ with the Ascension on the top. The speed with which the institution of marriage absorbed new ideas, such as Christianity, speaks to its flexibility.

B   A gold 4th-century Byzantine wedding ring carved to depict two facing busts. Christian attitudes towards marriage were often conflicted, and were shaped by Jewish, Roman and Greek thought and practice.

C   Mosaic depicting Empress Theodora and attendants (547). Emperor Justinian I married Theodora (500–48), a circus performer and sex worker, after changing a law banning high-ranking people marrying actresses.

As long as the sexual exploitation of slaves, concubines and sex workers was widely accepted, monogamy as a strict ideal of sexual morality would lack support. The emergence of the contemporary ideal, with its religious, moral and romantic connotations, was a long process, catalysed in the ancient world by the demise of slavery and the rise of Christianity. How did this process unfold, and how did monogamy spread globally?

Marital monogamy was required under Greek and Roman law, and it was within those contexts that increasingly elaborate and influential forms of Christian thought took hold. Initially, Christian thinking about monogamy was convoluted.

The Jewish tradition of the Old Testament had a place for polygyny (not polyandry), which was practised for procreation and prestige. Some church fathers, including Tertullian, regarded polygyny as a temporary exception from the monogamous rule, to help people 'be fruitful and multiply'. Others, such as St Augustine (354–430), who notoriously lived with a concubine for a time, thought that the coming of Christ altered the general procreative function of sex and marriage to the imitation of the relationship between Christ and his Church. Eventually, the church fathers developed a narrative of spiritual progress from polygamy towards monogamy and, ideally, to a state of chastity.

This early Christian context had an enduring influence, despite the fact that many of its practices and teachings assumed that the world was about to end. In his letter to the Corinthians, still often cited in marriages today, St Paul (*c.* 4 BC–*c.* AD 62/64) depicts marriage as the only acceptable context for sexual desire, but as inferior to celibacy. He takes a negative view of divorce, too, because he believed marriage had a sanctifying effect on spouses (even if pagan) and children. Paul's view is far removed from marriage as a practical union for mutual aid and stable property transfer.

Tertullian (*c.* 155–*c.* 220) was a north-African theologian and legal thinker whose writings came to define the early Christian Church. Mindful of the irony, he famously wrote a treatise called *On Patience*, which promoted the virtue he lacked most.

c

A

In Ephesians (5: 22 – 33), Paul also provided a statement of one of Christianity's most central and enduring metaphors: the Church as the bride of Christ. Viewed like this, spousal love in marriage symbolically evokes Christ's spiritual marriage to the Church; that is, an enduring, caring and sacrificial love. With this metaphor, monogamous marriage becomes a demanding and ideally permanent state.

By framing marriage in a spiritual context, Paul and other Christians transformed the monogamy ideal.

Furthermore, early Christians such as Paul thought in reasonably egalitarian ways. Although Paul was clear that the husband was 'the head of the wife as Christ is the head of the Church', he laid great emphasis on the need for husbands to love and respect their wives. This emphasis, and the practices of the early church in general, made (limited) space for women's perspective and experiences.

A   A 15th-century prayer book, probably created as a gift for a newly wed couple. Comparing the marital union to that between Christ and the Church helped to personalize the religious relationship, on the one hand, and spiritualize the marital relationship, on the other. But the comparison helped to entrench male dominance; women were always cast in the subordinate role.

B   This illuminated manuscript page shows the marriage of St Hedwig (1174–1243) to the Duke of Silesia (1165–1238). It nicely demonstrates the alignment between the interests of the Church and political power. The priest, Hedwig's father and the coterie of witnesses look happily upon the union.

B

Practically speaking, however, Christian thought on marriage was slow to develop and even slower to be institutionalized. Only after 1,000 years of Christianity do we see the increasing involvement of church institutions as a response to rising numbers of marital disputes, especially among powerful families and dynasties who had much to lose through bad marriages.

A

Decretum Gratiani is a collection of canon law texts compiled in the 12th century by theologian and jurist Gratian (dates unknown). Used by the Catholic Church until 1918, the *Decretum* attempted, albeit imperfectly, to coherently systematize existing laws, and influenced Christian attitudes to marriage.

The 12th-century compendium of canon law, known as the *Decretum Gratiani*, was the first systematic attempt to set out a consistent body of canon law that concerned, among other things, marriage and inheritance. The *Decretum* made consent and consummation prerequisites of marriage, thus shifting the legal focus from the power of families to individual intent and will. It was in this period, too, that polygamy was argued to be unnatural, spiritually harmful and socially dangerous. These divisive arguments, which instigated a long period of reform in the western Church, centred on the issue of clerical celibacy: on the right for priests to marry, or to live with concubines.

By the later Middle Ages, however, monogamy was entrenched as a spiritual and secular archetype. At the Council of Trent in 1563, the Catholic Church finally established marriage as a sacrament. Yet it was not until 1753 in England and Wales that marriages necessitated a formal ceremony in a church.

The ongoing development, consolidation and expansion of Christian concepts and institutions aided the dominance of monogamy.

Strict sexual monogamy, as a complement to marital monogamy, was a useful political tool. Early Christian societies sought to diverge from their Jewish origins, and, later, to oppose increasingly powerful Muslim polities on the fringes of a nascent empire. Stricter forms of monogamy helped forge a sense of moral and social identity through the 'othering' of social groups who practised polygamy. Early examples of these peoples were the Persians, Macedonians, Spartans, Celts and Germans. But throughout history, monogamy as a distinct mark of Christianity would be one of the ideological impositions of Western colonial expansion and missionary zeal around the world. The impact of these political projects is still being felt today, especially in Western Africa and parts of Asia where polygyny continues.

A   This majestic 15th-century altarpiece, by Rogier van der Weyden (1400–64), depicts all seven sacraments of the Roman Catholic Church: the eucharist, baptism, confirmation, confession, ordination, marriage and the last rites. A marriage is taking place on the right-hand panel.

B   Christian missionaries – like the ones in this 18th-century print – spread the doctrine and practices of their religion, including monogamy, throughout the world; at times riding on the coat-tails of colonial expansion, at times forging the way themselves. Polygamous communities were often highly resistant to their efforts.

A

A The topic of love assumed prominence in the court poetry of the European High Middle Ages, as illustrated in the *Great Heidelberg Book of Songs* (c. 1340). Love was something to be earned, not taken, and expressed ritualistically within a complex ethical framework.

B In the 18th century, elopements – as depicted in this etching from 1798 – became increasingly popular as marriages based on love alone were increasingly idealized.

This compressed history of the monogamy ideal neglects the importance of romantic love, but, like monogamy itself, the historical origins of our current fixation are complex. People have always had the capacity to care for and love each other, and evidence of loving unions is abundant throughout the past. Just because such love was valued, however, does not mean it motivated marital unions.

Indeed, one of our most culturally familiar tropes of 'romance' – knights, courtly gentility, honour and the damsel in distress – emerges from a medieval literary tradition in which love could only possible occur *outside* the bonds of marriage. True romantic love must be freely given, whereas married couples are duty bound to care for each other.

In his book *Love: A History* (2011), philosopher Simon May charts four historical developments in thought about love, from the elevation of love to supreme virtue in antiquity, to the ability to love through the grace of God, through to the idea that humans can be loved in themselves, to the modern thought that in loving we become our authentic selves.

With this trajectory in mind, it is better to regard the current esteem of romantic love as an ideological consequence of a social context where people are no longer firmly rooted in communities. We value love because we mostly live in industrial societies, with smaller kinship networks and an increased range of personal choice: contexts where mobility and individualism are the order of the day. It is no surprise that the 18th-century Romantic movement, and the cult of sentimentality, which catalysed a new fixation on romantic love, arose to prominence just as the Industrial Revolution gathered pace and ties with the land weakened.

The **Romantic movement** emerged at the end of the 18th century as an artistic and intellectual response to the rationalism of the Enlightenment and the disruptions of the Industrial Revolution. The Romantics valued emotional engagement with nature and social life.

The **Industrial Revolution** occurred between 1750 and 1850 as societies in Europe and North America shifted dramatically away from agrarianism. Inventions like steam power, the telegram and new forms of finance led to the mass production of goods and new forms of consumer culture.

B

A

It is unclear to what extent monogamy is a natural consequence of our evolution. It is best to understand monogamy's rise as a reaction to the structural features of a society, whether that is equalizing ratios of men to women, shifts from agricultural to wage labour, or reductions in inequalities of resources.

Once the monogamy ideal emerged, however, it persisted tenaciously, absorbing early Christian egalitarianism and new conceptions of romantic love, and outliving local efforts to reimpose polygamy.

B

A   These Valentine's Day cards, Victorian on the left, 1950s American on the right, show how ideals of romantic love vary dramatically between different historical and social contexts.

B   Although the romantic and domestic ideal of the 1950s lives on, the social and economic circumstances that made it practically possible have waned dramatically.

Although monogamy seemed rational and practicable to many people in the past, its continuing relevance is not guaranteed.

Monogamy's popularity does not mean it is always valuable, or that nonmonogamous relationships are flawed. The history of monogamy's origins should prompt caution. If society changes, or new norms emerge, this lingering fusion of Roman Law and Christian thinking, melded with romanticism, may, like polygyny, fall by the wayside.

2. Challenges to Monogamy

A

B

It is common to speak of 'monogamy in crisis'.

Recent statistics from the Organization for Economic Co-Operation and Development's (OECD) database are clear that, across the 36 member countries, compared to the 1970s, marriage rates are falling, divorce rates are rising and the average age of marriage is also rising. Against such changes, it is no surprise that some people feel that modern monogamy is demanding, and in tension with emerging ideals of personal growth, enriching experiences, dynamically negotiated relationships and an end to romantic complacency.

We must be cautious when speaking of monogamy under pressure, however, for it has always experienced tensions.

The **Organization for Economic Co-Operation and Development (OECD)** brings together 36 governments to promote global economic development and trade. It emerged from institutions established after the Second World War to help coordinate the redevelopment effort, and has since helped to collect data and institute trade agreements between member states.

The *Epic of Gilgamesh* is said to be the first work of literature, and is a long poem from Mesopotamia, in modern day Syria and Iraq. Written in the Sumerian language, it depicts the immortality-seeking escapades of Gilgamesh, part-God part-Man, and his initial rival and later friend Enkidu.

Instead we should ask what, if anything, is different about our current situation? Global contexts matter, too, as broad trends can mask the fact that monogamy manifests in different ways.

As an institution, monogamous marriage has always been in tension with humans' experiences of sexual desire, and infidelity is as old as marriage itself. In the *Epic of Gilgamesh* (*c.* 2150 – *c.* 1400 BC), for example, Gilgamesh refuses an offer of marriage from the goddess of love, Ishtar, because of her infidelities. Love, too, has been a longstanding threat to monogamy. The impact of this tension is a mainstay of literature, from *Romeo and Juliet* (*c.* 1595) by William Shakespeare (1564–1616) to *Madame Bovary* (1856) by Gustave Flaubert (1821–80), with many examples in between. The tension between dynastic interests and love has strained royal life, from Edward VIII (1894–1972) who abdicated the throne in 1936 to marry the divorcee Mrs Simpson (1896–1986), to the tensions that plagued Prince Charles's (b. 1948) marriage to Princess Diana (1961–97) in the 1980s and 1990s.

A   Some people worry that marriage has been trivialized in modern times. Marriages are certainly easier to get, quickly: at this chapel in Las Vegas, USA, weddings can be performed at a drive-through window.

B   Cupid's Wedding Chapel in Las Vegas, USA. In Roman mythology Cupid, the god of love and desire, was portrayed ambivalently: at times a benefactor, bestowing the gift of love on troubled mortals; at times devious, toying with people's feelings.

C   Tensions between sentiment and stability, desire and duty, are as old as marriage itself; but this would not have consoled King Edward VIII as he abdicated the throne to marry his love, the divorcee Wallis Simpson.

c

Historically, monogamy was also pressured by low life expectancies and the threat of death (especially to women in childbirth). Remarriage was a common response to loss in most early societies. It was only with the increasingly strict Christian focus on monogamous marriage that remarriage was viewed with hostility.

Infertility was another recurrent pressure on monogamous marriage because the preservation of power and property depended on the provision of heirs. Polygyny was occasionally permitted as a result, from the biblical tale of Abraham, Sarah and Hagar (also used to caution people about jealousy), to the Babylonian legal *Code of Hammurabi* (c. 1754 BC), which specified that if a man's wife was infertile, he could bring a second wife into the home on the condition that she 'not be allowed equality with his wife'.

A

A The ubiquity of death, and remarriage, in the 17th-century family is visible in this touching painting (c. 1636–7) by David Des Granges of Sir Richard Saltonstall's (1586–1661) family. Scholars think the painting depicts his deceased wife (in bed), his current wife and his children, one of whom also died.

B Industrialization, and changing social norms, enabled more people to treat the home as a space separate from the working world. It is no surprise, therefore, that new ideals of childhood, leisure activity and domestic taste were soon to emerge. These ideals were materialized in the vogue for elaborate doll's houses.

B

The **first demographic transition** happened when social rates of births and deaths fell significantly. Medical innovation prevented people from dying young and helped them control reproduction, thus making smaller families possible; while new ideas about childhood, family size and economic dependency made such families desirable.

Mortality and infertility only declined significantly with the Scientific and Industrial Revolutions of the mid-18th to mid-19th centuries (later in non-Western countries). Sociologists Ron Lesthaeghe and Dirk van de Kaa call this change the 'first demographic transition'.

Industrializing societies embraced new social norms. As children became less integral to the agricultural economy, the idea of an extended valuable childhood took hold in richer families; emerging consumerism, boosted by global trade, forged new connections between individual choice and quality of life; and the Romantic movement renewed focus on emotional life, in a century that ended with the American and French Revolutions.

These changes did not benefit everyone equally – the poor continued to suffer – but they consolidated over time. The meaning of 'until death do us part' changed as people lived longer, better lives. Unsurprisingly, perhaps, this period saw agitation for divorce reform. In this, England was an outlier, taking until 1857 to permit divorce on the ground of infidelity, cruelty or desertion. New divorce laws made serial monogamy more feasible and provided a legislative framework for the growing concern that marriages be amicable for wives and children.

A   In the early 20th century relations between the sexes and working-class culture both changed dramatically.
B   Members of the Women's Territorial Service kiss their partners before they leave for training in 1939.
C   British 'GI Brides' depart for America and a new life with their American husbands, after the Second World War.

The consolidation of this first major demographic transition saw further changes to social life and relationships, especially around the end of the 19th century.

A

Prior to the First World War, women were increasingly focusing on their personal freedom. Buoyed by the activism of first-generation feminists, popular culture fixated on sexuality and experimentation. The psychoanalytic theories of Sigmund Freud, with their ubiquitous sexual motives, were an invigorating conceptual background to the Roaring Twenties: an age of prosperity, jazz and flapper girls. This period saw the emergence of youth culture, cinematic visual culture and buoyant consumerism. People starting dating more casually, too, and in this they were aided by the motorcar, which increased mobility and broadened horizons. During this time, the distinction between the woman's private domestic sphere and the man's public political sphere, an ideal that had peaked under the Victorians, started to erode. Between 1880 and 1920, the chance of a marriage ending in divorce doubled from about one in twelve to one in six.

The Second World War further eroded the public / private distinction as many women had to enter the workforce, experiencing new freedoms. But despite a peak in divorce rates immediately after the war, with 4 divorces per 1,000 marriages in 1946 in the USA, compared to 2 per 1,000 in 1940, according to census data, the collective experience of war prompted a dramatic rise in marriages and the entrenchment of the ideal of the male breadwinner family.

First-generation feminists, or 'First Wave' feminists, were thinkers and activists after Mary Wollstonecraft (1759–97) who contested the unequal legal status of women, and who agitated for the vote in the 19th and early 20th century.

Sigmund Freud (1856–1939) was born in Vienna, and founded the practice of psychoanalysis to explore and treat various disorders.

Flapper girls challenged social norms of demure behaviour and restrained sexuality in the 1920s, and were known for their short skirts and hair.

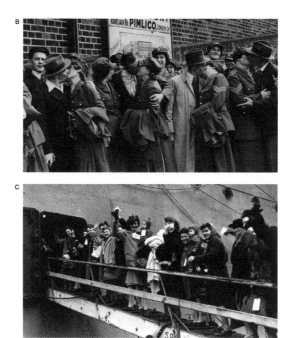

A After the chaos and terror of war, domestic life had a powerful appeal. It was not long before the ideal of 'home' was harnessed to elicit desire for new consumer appliances.

War trauma and the allure of domesticity led to this golden age of marriage. In the Allied countries, and other large economies like Japan, marriage was supported by policies aimed at rebuilding broken societies, such as the GI Bill of 1944 in the USA, which provided benefits to ex-soldiers. People began marrying much younger, and the divorce rate fell. In 1958, it was nearly half the 1947 rate, with around 370,000 divorces. Life expectancies increased too, which meant that people were spending longer portions of their life married. The post-war economic boom also increased domestic consumerism; new appliances promised a harmonious domestic life and better living standards.

For Lesthaeghe, the 1950s was also the start of a 'second demographic transition' in many countries in the industrialized world, in which people had fewer children, broke the link between marriage and family, embraced relationship and family forms other than marriage, and were geographically uprooted.

The **GI Bill** of 1944, officially named the Servicemen's Readjustment Act, did just that: help members of the Armed Forces in the USA adjust to life after the Second World War. It helped servicemen access mortgages and business loans, and covered the costs of university tuition and maintenance.

The **post-war economic boom** occurred between the end of the Second World War and the early 1970s as countries across the world experienced rapid and stable economic growth with high levels of employment.

The **second demographic transition** was driven by recent technological advances, such as the contraceptive pill, and normative changes, such as attitudes to cohabitation, homosexuality and relationships.

Second-wave feminists, such as Kate Millet (1934–2017), Germaine Greer (b. 1939) and Shulamith Firestone (1945–2012) were active around 1960, and were inspired by the civil rights movement to campaign for greater rights and equality for women, and an end to gender-based violence and discrimination.

The ideal of monogamous marriage reached its apogee in the 1950s, but dramatic social change would challenge married life like never before.

Some of the changes were economic. As the post-war boom faded, inflation in the 1970s eroded the value of the male breadwinner's wage, forcing more married women into work. The home was harder to maintain as an insulated domestic sphere as women were valued as employees, not merely as mothers and wives. Globalization meant workforces had to be increasingly flexible and mobile. Transience can make it harder to form a stable nuclear family as it is harder to find support from community or relatives.

Second-wave feminists challenged the patriarchalism that underpinned the post-war male breadwinner ideal, and campaigned for greater rights.

This sense of equality, coupled with a dawning awareness of the unhappiness and existential vacuity felt by many housewives, encouraged more women to return to work. Betty Friedan (1921–2006) labelled this unhappiness the 'problem that has no name' in her influential book *The Feminine Mystique* (1963), and it has been explored in art centring on this period of US social history, from the stories of Raymond Carver (1938–88), to Sue Kaufman's (1926–77) *Diary of a Mad Housewife* (1967), or the TV series *Mad Men* (2007–15).

The resurgent feminist movement also helped attack stigma surrounding divorce and fed into changing conceptions of a valuable life. Out went the notion that men and women had to adhere to well-defined social roles within a religious worldview, and in came the secularized idea that men and women could pursue their own lifestyles. The ideology of dissatisfied couples trying to 'make it work' arose alongside the liberalization of divorce law, which made exiting a relationship easier. However the ability to 'work at' relationships in innovative ways rather than simply leaving them, to make nuanced compromises or seek therapy, is easier if people have time and money, and so favours the socio-economically advantaged.

A

Swinger culture came to prominence with the free love movement of the 1960s. Swinging couples swap partners with each other or have group sex. Unlike polyamorists, swingers typically emphasise mutual friendship and sexual pleasure rather than pursuing multiple loving relationships.

A   Men and women bathing naked in a river at the first Woodstock festival in 1969. The rise of festival culture, with events like Woodstock, not only catalysed popular culture, but also appealed to some people as a model for wider, utopian social change.

B   Members of a 'free love' commune in Los Angeles in 1972. 'Free love' and swinging became more popular during the counter-cultural movement, in which people criticized political authority and military action, campaigned for civil rights and embraced experimental forms of life.

Slowly, people also started to accept other sexual orientations: a change of attitude that eventually led to marriage reforms in several countries (Denmark first legalized same-sex civil unions in 1989, whereas the Netherlands first legalized gay marriages in 2000). Same-sex marriage is now legal in 28 countries, from Iceland to New Zealand.

Perhaps the most dramatic change in romantic life was the introduction of the contraceptive pill in the early 1960s. Suddenly many women could control and delay reproduction. This technology catalysed the sexual revolution. When the risks of sex are reduced, it can be enjoyed more, and frequently, which enables people to explore their sexual identity.

The early 1970s saw forays into free love and the emergence of swinger culture, in which couples swap partners and experiment sexually (albeit without radically challenging monogamous marriage), as portrayed in *Bob & Carol & Ted & Alice* (1969), a successful comedy film about sexual experimentation.

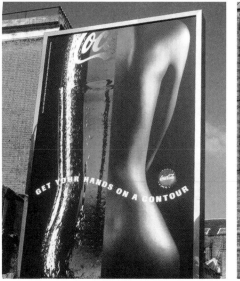

A

B

The sexual revolution was reflected in visual culture, too, as advertising, in particular, became increasingly sexualized. For instance the 1974 Weyenberg Massagic Shoe advert featured a naked women lying on the floor gazing at a shoe under the slogan 'Keep Her Where She Belongs'. Alongside sexualization, public awareness of diverse sexual identities and sexual minorities improved. Like all areas of modern life, the sexual revolution continued into the information age. Women, especially, were delaying marriage to find the 'right' partner, as they learnt more about their sexuality and started to value sexual experimentation, compatibility and fulfilment. In 2019 actress Emma Watson (b. 1990) made headlines by describing herself as 'self-partnered' – a rebuttal of the pressure she felt from society to be married by 30, and a reflection of the rise in 'single positivity'.

The social changes of the second demographic transition set the stage for the modern monogamy ideal, and the pressures we now experience.

A   The sexual revolution was quickly monetized, as the power of desire was harnessed to generate demand for products, underpinned by the misogynistic appeal of 'possession'.

B   This controversial 2010 advertisement for the underwear brand Sloggi shows the ongoing sexualization of women's bodies to fuel consumerism.

C   A Tinder advertisement reads 'single lives, as single wants.' Despite the promise of freedom and excitement, Internet dating results in insecurity for many.

Information technology – the Internet, smartphones, dating apps – allows the sexual revolution to continue with greater privacy and fewer risks. We can explore our sexual desires, join sexual subcultures and find partners with increasing ease. Similarly, Internet dating broadens romantic and sexual choice by helping us access numerous potentially compatible partners.

The **information age** means many countries now benefit from economies driven by information technology, such as computers, internet infrastructure and robotics. These technologies developed rapidly from the middle of the 20th century, and continue to do so.

An array of options increases the possibility that we could have chosen more wisely (hence why many people prefer restaurants with small menus). Internet dating can make us feel like we have many romantic 'options'. But this feeling, even if exaggerated, can fuel discontentment with a current partner as we imagine that there is someone more alluring, or more compatible, in cyberspace. This discontent, plus the ease with which we can now potentially meet new people, puts increasing pressure on the monogamy ideal.

c

A Since more women have entered the workplace and gained economic stability, more women have been having affairs. The reasons vary, but one is the desire to be fully appreciated.

B The wide range of intentions behind the use of dating apps is bound to lead to dissatisfaction and uncertainty, especially when desires are poorly articulated. For some, dating is an 'experience' in itself.

A

First, we might simply be bored, or worry we are missing out. Ashley Madison, the infidelity website, harnesses this worry with its slogan 'Life is short. Have an affair.' Some people turn to clandestine sex to address their boredom or curiosity, or to reconcile their desires for sexual variety, companionate love and domesticity. South Korea, the country with the highest degree of Internet connectivity, has vast rates of infidelity, with one study finding that more than 50% of married men had cheated. Demand for Ashley Madison's website surged after launching there.

Second, the prevalence and availability of other sources of romantic and sexual interest, from dating profiles to pornography, can introduce strands of jealousy or suspicion into our existing relationships. We could feel that our valued relationship is encircled by these alluring alternatives and feel insecure.

Monogamy is also pressured by the growing value of 'experiences' and excitement.

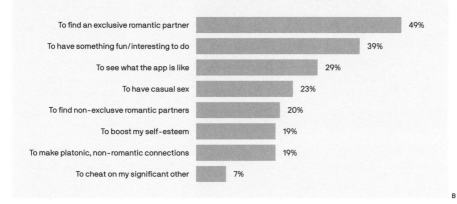

REASONS WHY USERS IN THE UNITED STATES USE DATING APPS AND WEBSITES
(JANUARY 2019)

To find an exclusive romantic partner	49%
To have something fun/interesting to do	39%
To see what the app is like	29%
To have casual sex	23%
To find non-exclusve romantic partners	20%
To boost my self-esteem	19%
To make platonic, non-romantic connections	19%
To cheat on my significant other	7%

B

This is perhaps a consequence of generational difficulties in accessing more conventional indicators of wealth (such as posessions or property), success and happiness, due to the ever-rising life expectancies of older generations. Many aspects of life, from possessions to events and relationships, are now evaluated in terms of their ability to elicit the right kinds of experience. The rising value of experience, as such, and the relationships that foster them, is bolstered by the waning of religious practice, and the erosion of families and community traditions.

We might think the rising value of close relationships is good for monogamy, but the nature of the desired relationship has itself changed as a result of the ongoing sexual revolution and the democratization of social life. Because we want different things in this age, satisfying romantic relationships are harder to find, and we are more sensitive to romantic potential outside of a relationship.

A

B

A   A matchmaking fair in Beijing, China, organized by the country's biggest matchmaking website. Online matchmaking is big business. It typically retains an explicitly monogamous focus, the idea being that individuals can have a vastly expanded field of choice whilst still seeking 'the one'.

B   Male participants at a mass matchmaking event in Shanghai, China. Exposure to so many potential partners may make partners more aware of the contingenices of romantic love, or alternatively reinforce monogamous ideals.

C   In many respects Valentine's Day celebrations remind us of the enduring power of both the monogamous ideal, and the privileging of romantic love over other kinds of relationship (amatonormativity).

The changing expectations of romantic life have been captured by sociologist Anthony Giddens. In *The Transformation of Intimacy* (1992), he argued that, as part of a 'generic restructuring of intimacy' people now seek the 'pure relationship'; that is, 'a social relation is entered into for its own sake, for what can be derived from each person from a sustained association with another; and which is continued only in so far as it is thought by both parties to deliver enough satisfactions to stay within it.' Seen this way, relationships involve the attempt to insert the 'self and other into a personal narrative which has no particular reference to wider social practices'. Relationships are now seen as direct sources of meaning.

Giddens thinks we want our relationships to be driven by 'confluent love', which is an 'opening oneself out to the other', which is 'active [and] contingent'. Confluent love 'presumes equality in emotional give and take' and will only develop 'to the degree to which each partner is prepared to reveal concerns and needs to the other and to be vulnerable to that other'.

Confluent love is not necessarily sexually exclusive.

Sexual monogamy 'has a role in the relationship to the degree to which the partners mutually deem it desirable or essential'. Monogamy has new significance for those who seek pure relationships animated by confluent love, personality and passion. Although some still view monogamy as a refuge from social change, for others, monogamy is now an optional arrangement, requiring justification, which must reflect the authentic selves of both partners.

As more people value pure relationships, the monogamy ideal becomes more demanding. Mere fidelity is not enough. People want to find 'the one': the person with whom their desires, values and emotions resonate completely. As clinical psychologist Michael Vincent Miller writes in his book *Intimate Terrorism: The Deterioration of Erotic Life* (1995): 'What heroic performances the partners in a couple must feel they have to turn in! They have to be sexual athletes, parents to the child in each other, perfect friends [and] therapists to one another's symptoms.'

c

A The rise of marriage counselling coincided with the rise of new romantic norms, as new tools were sought to achieve increasingly valued emotional intimacy.
B Amazon founder Jeff Bezos and his ex-wife MacKenzie, who whose 2019 divorce was the most expensive in history.

These new tensions pressure monogamy. Infidelity can now look like a 'solution' to a broader range of 'problems', not simply a lack of sexual pleasure, but as offering intimate fulfilment, the 'experience' of variety or the possibility of having one's authentic self 'seen' by another.

Similarly, because people want more from relationships, they are less likely to settle early, especially as casual dating, late marriage and cohabitation are now common. These social and ideological changes produce pressure towards serial monogamy. People explore relationships before moving on because they are reluctant to accept less than what the new monogamy ideal demands.

The ideal of confluent love between two emotionally resonant partners also arguably outruns many people's ability to communicate well. Tensions arise when people endorse a demanding vision of good relationships, while lacking the means to maintain them. This is partly a generational tension.

Children of the second demographic transition, raised on the emotionally demanding variant of monogamy, have more traditional parents. Younger people may lack examples of confluent modes of communication, in which partners articulate their desires, values, and feelings out of a commitment to a robust and dynamic intimacy. Their parents are more likely to view relationships in terms of social roles, duties and expectations. Couples today are less likely to accept marriages like that of Tom and Daisy in *The Great Gatsby* (1925), Basil and Sybil in *Fawlty Towers* (1975–79) or Frank and April in *Revolutionary Road* (1961) – which conform to social expectations and have practical benefits whilst being devoid of care or meaningful communication. The struggle for modern romantic flourishing begins in the middle of the story.

Finally, it is vital to note how modern monogamy may impact families. Many marriages end in divorce, and some break-ups are related to the demanding norms of romantic intimacy, or the fear of missing out (sexually, or otherwise) as people live longer. Separations introduce stress and uncertainty into children's lives. Parents' subsequent dating, or the addition of new partners into a family, can also be disruptive. Even marriages that avoid divorce can impact children's lives with jealousy or midlife crises.

Generational tensions often concern wealth and political values, since older generations are more likely to have accumulated wealth at the expense of younger ones. These tensions are frequently reflected in political allegiances, with older voters preferring conservative parties and younger voters favouring progressive parties.

B

A   Nadia, an Afghan woman seeking a divorce from her abusive husband in 2017: something unthinkable for many women in Afghanistan. 70–80% of women there face forced marriage, and in 2008 it was found that nearly 90% of women had experienced domestic abuse.

B   The ability to end a relationship is especially important for women, who have historically been oppressed through monogamous marriages. As we have seen, monogamous and patriarchal ideas have usually coexisted. A growing number of woman in Afghanistan, like Nadia, are seeking divorce as a form of empowerment. However, this is a difficult path and they still face many oppressions.

C   The erosion of traditional social bonds, coupled with the greater prominence placed on intimacy, can leave some people feeling isolated. Here people find some solace in a Japanese 'cuddle café'.

Monogamy becomes harder to endorse uncritically as more people value self-assertion, sexual exploration, democratic communication, personal experience and equality of opportunity.

The second demographic transition is not uniform. In many societies these changes are nascent so we must not suppose that marriage and family structures are the same everywhere.

In his book *Between Sex and Power: Family in the World, 1900–2000* (2004) sociologist Göran Therborn argues that we should not suppose that forms of intimate and family life are straightforwardly converging around the world. In India, for instance, arranged or semi-arranged marriages remain common, while in Japan there is a growing industry for renting a family member or partner for a short-term period.

Therborn identifies seven distinct 'family-sex-gender-generation' systems: the Christian-European, the Islamic West Asian/North African, the South Asian, the Confucian East Asian, the sub-Saharan African, the Southeast Asian and the Creole. Globally, family systems exist which reject individual partner choice and the notion of the pure relationship.

The worry that monogamy is limiting is unlikely to resonate with people in societies that have not experienced the social changes of the second demographic transition, and their attendant impact on romantic ideals. Whether these changes will come, and whether they will destabilize monogamous norms as they are currently doing so in the West, is unclear.

The emerging ideals of mutually negotiated relationships, emotional vulnerability and personal growth have not toppled the 1950s ideal of the monogamous nuclear family. But that ideal presupposes a mode of socio-economic life that few societies can now sustain. These tensions prompt a search for solutions, some of which we consider in Chapter 3.

An **arranged marriage** is a marriage organized by people other than the couple themselves, usually their parents or wider community. There are a variety of arranged marriage traditions and practices worldwide.

c

新感覚の癒しビジネス
ソイネ屋2号店が新宿にオープン

3. Revisiting Monogamy

A People can be
   disoriented by
   the gap between
   the ideal and the
   reality of monogamous
   relationships, a reality
   with moments of
   boredom, complacency,
   or poor communication.
B An emphasis on
   initial compatibility
   between monogamous
   partners can detract
   from the ongoing
   practices of listening,
   communicating
   and accommodation
   in romantic life.

Monogamy is under pressure in modern life. The ideal partner can seem elusive as we live longer, seek variety and strive for love which engages our authentic selves. If we are single, we might search restlessly for love, simultaneously bewildered by the fecundity of dating apps yet reluctant to settle. Serial monogamy may be our fate as we drift romantically. If we are already partnered, we may torturously compare our situation to the modern monogamy ideal. Does our partner *totally* get us, *really* share our values, *truly* understand our feelings, *fully* satisfy us sexually? As the voices of doubt get louder, we may risk an affair, whether sexual or emotional, or seek solace elsewhere. If the voices are too loud, we may end our relationship and gamble on finding fulfilment elsewhere.

There are three broad ways to respond to the pressured world of modern monogamy.

First, we could try harder to meet the high standards of modern romance. Second, we could adjust our personal expectations of relationships, and reimagine the institution of marriage. Third, we could explore alternatives to monogamy, such as open relationships or polyamory.

Many people like the modern monogamy ideal. It promises intimate partnerships based on shared values, respect, understanding, and emotional harmony, which form the foundation of small loving families. So perhaps people just need to work on themselves and their relationships. This could involve therapy, as individuals or couples, to explicitly explore impediments to intimacy. Simmering conflicts, silent resentment, neglected trauma, bad habits, poor communication, feelings of inferiority, anxiety, insecurity, jealousy, anger and much else can fester at the heart of a relationship, making it difficult for partners to connect. Therapy, or its noninstitutional equivalents – talking with friends, reading books or learning from community groups or religious communities – can help people address these barriers.

A A challenge for
   any relationship
   is that people differ
   significantly, change
   over time and know
   themselves imperfectly.
B Passionate love trumps
   domestic harmony
   in Noël Coward's play,
   Private Lives (1930).
   Elyot and Amanda,
   whose stormy
   relationship ended
   in divorce five years
   earlier, discover they
   cannot live without
   each other when
   they find themselves
   staying in adjacent
   rooms at the same
   hotel, each with
   their new spouses.

But sometimes our efforts are not completely effective.
Challenging feelings and habits may resist therapy, or
we may simply find our love waning over time. Perhaps
scientific advances can help us here, instead. In their book
Love Drugs: The Chemical Future of Relationships (2020),
philosophers Brian D. Earp and Julian Savulescu explore
the possibility that couples may be able to use existing
substances, from oxytocin sprays and therapeutic
MDMA (the active ingredient in ecstasy) to enhance
romantic intimacy or deepen attachment over time.
In case this seems like cheating, remember that we
already modify our environments and our biochemistry
in the service of romance. A daily spritz of oxytocin maybe
an alternative to a weekly candle-lit dinner with a bottle
of Pinot Noir or some over-the-counter Viagra. The use
of love drugs may pose new ethical questions, but if these
can be answered it could provide an additional tool in
meeting the demands of the modern monogamy ideal.

A second approach to
the pressures of modern
monogamy is to revise our
expectations. Attention to
the historical development
of monogamy should
encourage us to be more
realistic about romantic
life, especially marriage.

Oxytocin sprays contain a hormone produced in the brain which is associated with social bonding. As a medication it can be used to induce labour, but most attention focuses on its purported ability to foster close bonds as a 'love drug', or to help people with depression.

MDMA, scientifically named 3,4-Methylenedioxy methamphetamine, is a psychoactive drug used to induce feelings of energy, pleasure and closeness to other people. Use of the drug is associated with electronic music and rave culture.

Such realism should involve an awareness of the abiding differences between loving spouses and how desires and projects change over time. Helena Bonham Carter (b. 1966) and Tim Burton's (b. 1958) unique approach to their relationship, for instance, saw them living for thirteen years in separate yet conjoined houses. Gwyneth Paltrow (b.1972) and Brad Falchuk (1971) also resisted the traditional relationship-escalator by keeping separate houses for a year after their marriage.

Personally, we should recognize that the desire for a pure relationship, animated by love and equality, can often obscure the practicalities of sustaining an extended partnership. Relationships based on the experience of deep reciprocal intimacy alone can be fragile, especially as we live in societies which still presuppose male domination. In acknowledging this, we can adjust our aspirations, recognize the practical aspects of relationships, and commit, with humility, to realistic processes of communication.

B

Realism about marriage may be promoted by the state enacting laws to reflect its actual social status as one relationship type among others, and laws that focus on what is central to any good close relationship: namely, care.

In her book *Minimizing Marriage (2012)*, philosopher Elizabeth Brake argues that the state should replace traditional marriage with 'minimal marriage'. This would be a legally recognized status to protect people in caring relationships, whether or not they are romantic, sexual, heterosexual, monogamous or involve children. Caring involves attending to material needs and providing emotional support.

A

A In recent decades, arguments for same-sex marriage have often appealed to consistency. If heterosexual relationships should be protected because they foster care and stability, then any relationship which fosters the same goods should also be protected, hence why same-sex marriage should be legal.

B Three men who gained legal recoginition as the first 'polyamorous family' in Columbia in 2017. One reason to think non-normative forms of care should be protected by the state is that care has traditionally been gendered female. This stereotype reinforces patriarchal norms and impoverished ideals of masculinity, so we should support non-stereotypical relationships.

C A 'just married' card for three Columbian men adapts an old tradition to a new reality. Plural marriage activists argue that if heterosexual marriages are recognized because they foster care and stability, then governments should recognize any relationship which fosters the same goods.

B

C

Minimal marriages would still have a contract-like form and a distinct social status to distinguish them from other interpersonal relationships, making them special to people and their communities. Monogamous marriage, as such, however, would no longer be privileged. People could legally protect any caring relationship irrespective of its form, including caring group relationships.

The focus on care ensures minimal marriages cannot be too big. We could not marry all of our 'friends' on social media, for example, because we cannot form a close caring relationship with so many people at once. Children would benefit, as minimal marriages recognize and protect people who provide continuity of care for others, but they would also allow larger care networks with multiple recognized contributors to be formed.

A

Brake's view is motivated by two central thoughts. The first is that caring relationships are a genuine primary good. Whatever life we want, whatever we do or value, we need care. Children need to be cared for when developing, and adults need care throughout life. Brake's second thought is that the state makes an unjustifiable value judgment about the good life for citizens if its marriage laws focus on a different social status, such as heterosexual romantic relationships, or exclude genuinely caring but nonsexual relationships, such as asexual relationships.

Primary good was defined by the political philosopher John Rawls (1921–2002) as something which someone needs as a citizen, in order to pursue their life and become reasonable and rational. Primary goods include basic rights and freedoms, some income, and social recognition.

Asexual means to not experience sexual attraction to other people. Asexuals may experience arousal, have sex and have romantic relationships. It is not chosen, like celibacy, or experienced as a harmful absence, like a desire disorder.

Heteronormative societies treat heterosexuality and its associated gender and family roles as the default. Queer people typically face discrimination in such societies.

A **bundle of rights** are conferred in one go through the acquisition of a social role or status, for example by becoming a judge or by marrying, rather than being acquired incrementally. This means some people acquire rights they do not need, and others may struggle to access a specific right without acquiring the whole package.

Instituting Brake's vision of minimal marriage would require sweeping change. Her approach alters the default form of state-recognized relationships. This would prompt more people to question whether they want a traditional union or something different. The move to minimal marriage also places flexibility at the heart of how the state protects relationships; it would show that the state is serious about protecting relationships insofar as they are caring, but without presupposing or privileging the monogamous, heteronormative, male breadwinner nuclear family. In moving to minimal marriage, the state encourages realism about relationships.

More radically, however, we might think the best way to foster realistic expectations about romantic relationships is for states not to recognize them at all. Philosopher Clare Chambers, in her book *Against Marriage* (2017), argues that marriage is always a harmful union because it sustains inequalities by privileging one type of relationship over others. Legal institutions of marriage require people to opt in to acquire rights. If they opt in, by marrying, they benefit from a bundle of rights (more than 1,000 statutory provisions in the USA) irrespective of whether they need them. Chambers thinks this situation is discriminatory.

Although the bundling of rights is convenient for states, bundling is blind to the complexity of many modern relationships and expresses implicit value judgments. The fact that the default situation requires people to opt in to acquire rights may also harm the vulnerable: people who, for whatever reason, are unwilling or unable to opt in. Cohabiting co-parents, for example, may find themselves in relationships functionally identical to married people, without their benefits.

From 2020 it will be possible in the UK for heterosexual couples to enter into a civil partnership instead of a marriage. This offers an option for those wishing to enjoy the legal benefits of marriage, but without the religious and patriarchal baggage that many see as attached to the term. It does still require an opt-in to acquire the rights and benefits, however.

A

Civil partnerships are legally recognized relationships between people. They confer rights and responsibilities similar to those associated with marriage, but lack religious significance. Civil partnerships may be favoured by people who resist the historical connotations of marriage.

A   Campaigners recently won an extension of civil partnerships to heterosexual couples in England and Wales. They argued that legislation governing relationships should not discriminate on grounds of gender or sexual orientation.

B   YouTubers Tana Mongeau and Jake Paul help us note the difference between marriage as a status and as a legal category. They traded enormously on being 'married', but their union was not legal.

B

Chambers envisages a situation in which states drastically change the default. Anyone who occupies a certain functional relationship: caregiver, parent, co-owner of a house and so on, should automatically be protected by the state by virtue of having that status. (They can opt out if they like.) In this view, there are no marriages. People could call themselves married and have elaborate ceremonies, but their unions would have no legal status. Indeed, modern marriage can be more centred on pomp and ceremony rather than legality anyway, with popular reality TV series *Don't Tell the Bride* enchanting audiences with spectacular weddings that are not legally binding, and influencers such as Tana Mongeau and Jake Paul live streaming their extravagant weddings whilst never making them legal.

Perhaps the best way to foster a realistic monogamy ideal is to make all romantic relationships personal.

A A road sign in Kentucky, USA. Religious norms still impact how the state views relationships and marriage, and so shape the lives of many, even in countries like the USA where state and church are constitutionally separated.
B The flag for asexual pride. The black represents asexuality, the grey demisexuality, the white allies and the purple community.
C A black ring worn on the middle finger is used by many asexual people as a symbol of their asexuality, and as a way of feeling part of a community.

A

The marriage-free state expresses no view about specific relationships. When no relationships are privileged, people have greater freedom to decide how to live. They may want to 'marry' for personal reasons, to respect religious faith or affirm commitment to family, but that would not be something that gifts them a special legal status. When relationship choice is personal, people are arguably more likely to pursue a form of life that suits them and their partner(s), rather than one that meets an existing standard or is well-supported by tax breaks and legal protections. Abolishing marriage could give people greater ownership of their romantic life.

A third option open to people who are wary of modern monogamy is to explore nonmonogamy. There are several kinds of nonmonogamous relationship, but they are all alike in not restricting romantic and sexual life to one person at a time.

People want to pursue nonmonogamy for many reasons. A person in a committed relationship might want to act on an existing attraction or love for someone else rather than deny their feelings. Such a person could end their current relationship and pursue the other person, to cheat on their current partner (sexually or emotionally) or to explore nonmonogamy. Such an example raises thorny issues around consent and proper respect for the existing partner, but nonmonogamy gives people the option, at least, to avoid compromising their feelings in an honest way.

Not everyone experiences attraction, desire and intimacy in the same way or to the same extent, so nonmonogamy can also help people accommodate personal differences. Asexual people (who do not experience sexual attraction) in relationships with people who experience sexual attraction (allosexuals) may want their partners to be sexually satisfied if they do not have sex together. Similarly, someone who is not particularly romantic may want their partner to enjoy that aspect of romantic life with someone else.

B

C

A

Some people simply want an unrestricted romantic life. They may be motivated by ethical reasons and see nonmonogamy as a practical alternative to contemporary romantic norms. Alternatively, they might enjoy variety and see no issue with the desire to have several mutually consenting relationships. Or they may doubt they are likely to find 'the one' person who completely satisfies them, or doubt they could be 'the one' for someone else. Perhaps they place high value on affection and intimacy, and want more loving interaction than one busy person could reasonably provide. If they are bi- or pansexual, and experience attraction to people of different genders, then nonmonogamy can enable them to act on their attractions. Lovers of excitement in romantic life may actively value nonmonogamy's potential for intrigue and sexual tension. Similarly, someone might view nonmonogamous life as an opportunity for personal growth, perhaps a way of confronting difficult emotions such as jealousy.

Pansexual people can experience sexual attraction to others irrespective of their sexual or gender identity. Pansexuals often distinguish themselves from bisexuals, who are attracted to men and women, in stressing the fluidity of their attractions.

A Participants at a fashion show run by the famous fetish club Torture Garden, London. Nonmonogamy can help some people express themselves sexually. This can be particularly important for women and sexual minorities, whose sexuality and sexual autonomy has been devalued historically.

B Women from the Killing Kittens community, a members-only club that hosts female-centred sex parties. While one strand of nonmonogamy is individualistic, with people placing emphasis on individual freedom, self-expression and excitement, another strand emphasizes community, solidarity and care.

Finally, nonmonogamy can help some people access more useful resources in life. The more relationships a person has, the more love, care, support, financial help, practical assistance, child support and knowledge they can draw upon. If this is true of friends and family, it may also be true of romantic partners. Indeed, since romantic partners are often close intimates they can arguably offer more of these resources, in more areas of life, than friends and family. Virginia Woolf's (1882–1941) sister Vanessa Bell's (1879–1961) open marriage to Clive Bell (1881–64) was described by one of her lovers, Roger Fry (1866–1934), as 'a triumph of reasonableness over the conventions', allowing them to both take multiple lovers and remain close friends throughout their lives.

B

A

Orientation, in the sexual sense, describes the predominate pattern of someone's attractions to other people. Lesbians, for example, are women who are typically sexually attracted to other women. Recent research into orientation, identity and behaviour is revealing how flexible sexual attraction can be.

Relationship anarchy involves trying to resist many monogamous and heteronormative norms and ideals. Relationship anarchists reject possessiveness and ownership, the institution of marriage and hierarchies between different kinds of relationships, such as friendships and sexual relationships, and prize individual autonomy.

For some nonmonogamous people, the value of increased resources is especially important when it comes to childcare. For them, the nuclear unit may seem stifling and limited, and broader romantic care networks, whether based in a communal living context or extended over a community, are preferable. Indeed, an African proverb states that 'it takes a village to raise a child', acknowledging the large number of people involved in the healthy and happy development of children. Whether those people are extended family, a local community or a polyamorous group is less important.

Nonmonogamous life has such a distinct appeal to some people that it has been said to be an **orientation**, like being gay. This is the view taken by legal scholar Ann Tweedy in her article 'Polyamory as a Sexual Orientation' (2010). She observes that some forms of nonmonogamy are highly embedded in people's lives and structure their values, and that these people would benefit from anti-discrimination laws, like other sexual minorities.

Although nonmonogamy is central to some people's identities, sociologist Christian Klesse urges caution when it comes to the claim that this is an orientation, rather than a preference. In his article 'Polyamory: Intimate Practice, Identity or Sexual Orientation?' (2014) he notes that orientation discourse often entrenches categories in ways that obscure complicated patterns of love and desire. As he puts it: 'The equation of polyamory with sexual orientation may undermine the disruptive potential of the category polyamory, achieve only selective protection under the law, obstruct the ability of poly movements to pursue broader alliances and foster a politics of recognition at the expense of a more transformative political agenda.'

There are many different kinds of sexual and romantic identities. But we can usefully distinguish between three core types of nonmonogamy – open relationships, polyamory and relationship anarchy – while recognizing other variants and categories are possible in between.

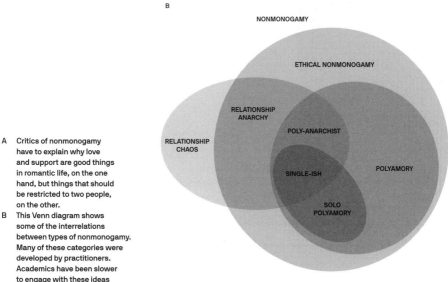

A   Critics of nonmonogamy have to explain why love and support are good things in romantic life, on the one hand, but things that should be restricted to two people, on the other.

B   This Venn diagram shows some of the interrelations between types of nonmonogamy. Many of these categories were developed by practitioners. Academics have been slower to engage with these ideas and their implications.

B

NONMONOGAMY

ETHICAL NONMONOGAMY

RELATIONSHIP
ANARCHY

POLY-ANARCHIST

RELATIONSHIP
CHAOS

SINGLE-ISH

POLYAMORY

SOLO
POLYAMORY

We can understand the differences between these relationship types in reference to monogamy's defining features: monosexuality, monoamory and partisanship. All nonmonogamous relationships invert at least one of these dimensions, and some invert them all.

People who have open relationships typically have a loving bond with one person while having sex with other people. They embrace polysexuality while retaining monoamory. This kind of relationship will appeal to people who enjoy sexual variety, experience discrepancies in sexual desire, value exclusive love or who do not want to invest time in maintaining other forms of intimacy.

A

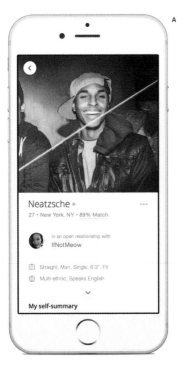

Neatzsche •   •••
27 • New York, NY • 89% Match

In an open relationship with
IfNotMeow

Straight, Man, Single, 6'3", Fit
Multi-ethnic, Speaks English

⌄

My self-summary

Monosexuality is defined by Meg-John Barker in their book *Rewriting the Rules* (2012) as people who do not have sex with, or experience significant sexual attraction toward, more than one person. In different contexts it may also mean people attracted to only one gender.

Monoamory means to only love, or experience an emotionally close relationship with, one person. The opposite of monoamory is polyamory, where people may love several people.

Partisanship is used in this book to label a spectrum of allegiance to a romantic partner. Highly partisan partners will be closed-off to the romantic or sexual aspects of other people. Less partisan partners will be open to others in these ways.

B

The practicalities of opening up a relationship may be difficult to navigate, as empathetically demonstrated in the 2018 TV drama *Wanderlust*, however when the process is well managed, the result can clearly be rewarding: the existentialist philosophers Jean-Paul Sartre and Simone de Beauvoir had an open marriage for over 50 years.

In contrast, people in polyamorous relationships are open to the idea of having several concurrent loving relationships, which may or may not have a sexual dimension. Polyamory will appeal to people who value love, find love easy to experience and have the practical and emotional resources required to devote time to several people. Polyamory is often viewed as emotionally demanding because the intimacy involved is greater, as is the potential for the integration of multiple lives. For example, Professor William Moulton Marston (1893–1947), creator of the Wonder Woman comics, lived in a three-way polyamorous relationship with his wife Elizabeth (1893–1993) and research assistant Olive Byrne (1904–85). He had two children with each woman, and they all lived together as a family. In situations like this, it is less easy to 'insulate' a core relationship from the influence of other people, which could make jealousy more prevalent.

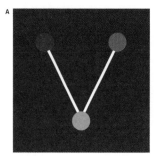
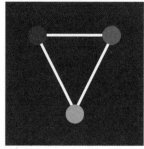
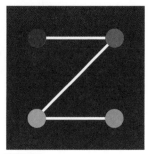

V TYPE   TRIANGLE / TRIAD TYPE   Z / N TYPE

Both open relationships and polyamory typically involve some kind of hierarchy between those involved. Some people talk in terms of 'primary' and 'secondary' partners, where primary partners take precedence over secondary ones, perhaps by having their relationship recognized in marriage; others make a distinction between the person or people they live with, and those relationships without a domestic aspect. Still others may only do certain activities with one partner and not another, such as going on holiday, sharing childcare responsibilities or having unprotected sex. These rules are intended to structure romantic life.

A   As these diagrams illustrate, the internal structure of nonmonogamous relationships can vary dramatically. These differences are not obscure, however; they are comparable to how different groups of friends relate. Some friendship groups are close and reciprocal, others form looser networks where people do not share friends of friends.

Relationship anarchists, in contrast to both people in open relationships and the polyamorous, embrace polysexuality and polyamory, and aspire to be extremely nonpartisan. For them, the idea of a 'secondary' partner is demeaning, and the attempt to enforce hierarchies of relationships risks entrenching 'amatonormativity' – where amorous (romantically loving) relationships are socially privileged. Relationship anarchists think all relationships, whether sexual or not, loving or not, are important and have value. As the originator of the term, Andie Nordgren, states: 'Relationship anarchy questions the idea that love is a limited resource that can only be real if restricted to a couple.... Don't rank and compare people and relationships – cherish the individual and your connection to them.'

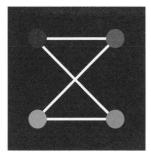
HOURGLASS TYPE

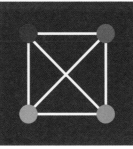
QUAD TYPE

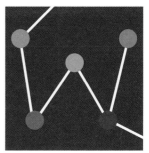
WEB TYPE

These three forms of nonmonogamy share some values, which help distinguish them from avowed monogamous people who have illicit affairs. In her influential article 'Monogamy's Law' (2004), legal scholar Elizabeth Emens suggests the following five principles are central to polyamory (and arguably to nonmonogamy more generally): self-knowledge, radical honesty, consent, self-possession and the privileging of love and sex. To these we can add the norm of distinct, clear and nonaggressive communication. These values may be shared by some monogamous people, too, especially those who embrace the ideal of confluent love, but they form an explicit aspect of nonmonogamous discourse, both among theorists and in the daily lives of those who negotiate multiple relationships.

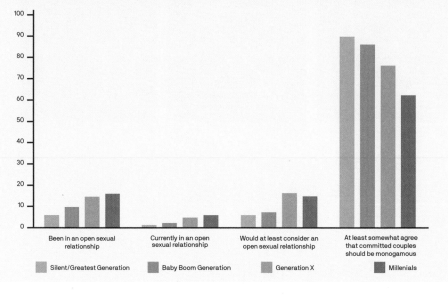

GENERATIONAL DIFFERENCES IN CONSENSUAL NONMONOGAMY BEHAVIOURS AND ATTITUDES (2018)

Been in an open sexual relationship | Currently in an open sexual relationship | Would at least consider an open sexual relationship | At least somewhat agree that committed couples should be monogamous

Silent/Greatest Generation   Baby Boom Generation   Generation X   Millenials

A

Many nonmonogamous people have families. Their specific family dynamic will depend on the kind of nonmonogamy they pursue, how many children they have, the age of their children and whether they share domestic space. The fundamentalist Mormon groups in the USA with multiple wives and up to 20 children will look very different to the families in rural Tibet practicing fraternal polyandry (one woman marrying multiple brothers). In her study of polyamorous families *The Polyamorists Next Door* (2013), Elisabeth Sheff notes that many polyamorous people involve their partners as active co-parents to take advantage of the extra emotional and practical resources. But other nonmonogamous people, perhaps those with open relationships, may have a 'conventional' dual or single parent domestic life that is kept separate from their romantic life.

To some people, nonmonogamy has appeal in the wake of the sexual revolution, and as the second demographic transition gathers pace, changing how people live, when and if they marry, and how they raise a family. But others view nonmonogamy with suspicion.

A Openness to nonmonogamy seems to correlate with age. This fact will be explained by many factors, but one will be how younger people have experienced their parents' relationships.
B A man watches television with his two wives and nine of their ten children in Centennial Park, a polygamist community on the border of Utah and Arizona, USA. To consider nonmonogamy seriously, we have to resist the influence of negative stereotypes. This helps us recognize the diversity of nonmonogamous relationships, and understand how prejudice can mask genuine goods and values.

From a monogamous perspective, non-monogamous relationships can seem incompatible with deep intimacy or specialness; liable to generate conflict or jealousy; and incompatible with raising a family. Even supporters of nonmonogamous relationships may pause before suggesting plural marriages should be allowed. In Chapter 4, we consider whether these suspicions are justified.

B

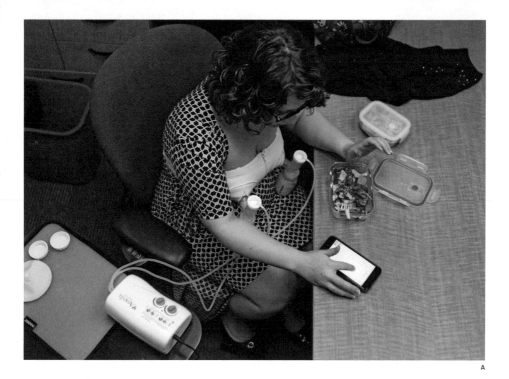

No intimate relationship is immune from problems, but nonmonogamous relationships are commonly held to be more problematic than others, as harmful, impractical or in tension with human nature. A closer look at some criticisms of nonmonogamy helps to dispel common myths about these relationships and better understand the issues they can generate. Chapter 4 will focus on polyamory, because it is often regarded as the most demanding version of nonmonogamy.

Polyamory is often thought to be impractical for individuals and as a context in which to raise a family. We might think that if we have more than one romantic relationship then there will not be enough time, energy or money to be shared between everyone, that we will be spread too thinly and neglect important obligations.

A   A woman juggles work, lunch and childcare. All relationships, especially those involving children, and no matter their form, involve a complex balance of prioritization, compromise and sacrifice.

B   Calendars, schedules, organization: they are part of modern life irrespective of how, or who, we love. How these demands are managed is usually more important than where they come from.

It is important to care for the people who depend on us. But is polyamory more impractical, in this respect, than other forms of life? Monogamous people can have demanding careers, a family, friends, hobbies and political interests, and have to make difficult choices about what to prioritize; indeed, monogamous life can easily become more impractical than nonmonogamous life.

Prioritization is part of any relationship, but the polyamorous emphasis on honesty and ongoing explicit communication can enable people to acknowledge and address potential tensions in a realistic way.

B

A   Protesters of the Gay Marriage Bill in the UK, in 2013. Objectors to non-normative romantic relationships often presuppose heteronormative family ideals.

B   Masked supporters of an anti-gay marriage movement in Paris, France, protest against medically assisted procreation.

Many people worry, however, that polyamory cannot provide an appropriate environment in which to raise children. In his book *Cheap Sex: The Transformation of Men, Marriage, and Monogamy* (2017), sociologist Mark Regnerus voices this concern: 'A polyamorous life is only conceivable when no one actually conceives.' Similarly, the research mentioned in Chapter 1 seems to suggest monogamous families are clearly preferable to nonmonogamous families. Interestingly, however, the emerging empirical research into the impact of polyamory on children suggests that polyamory may actually provide benefits for families, and that the pitfalls of polyamory are either shared with modern monogamous families or are the consequence of hostile social attitudes.

Elisabeth Sheff's book *The Polyamorists Next Door* (2013) provides the most comprehensive analysis of the impact of polyamory on families. Using close observation and interviews, she identifies some potential pitfalls of this lifestyle. The first group of pitfalls consists of the experience of stigma, potential social rejection and institutional vulnerability.

A

In a society that is hostile to nonmonogamy, polyamorous parents and their children may experience traumatic stigma and social rejection. Even worse, polyamorous families may encounter institutional prejudice, with judges and social workers making assumptions about people's parental abilities based on their romantic life. In her article 'Monogamy's Law' (2004), for example, Elizabeth Emens documents a case in which a judge removed legal custody from a woman who openly had two partners, on the grounds that this showed she was a poor parent. Emens quotes the judge: 'When some guy came to her and said I'm in love with you too although you are married, you know, most people would have said, well, hey, I'm married; forget it. But, no, she decides, well, why not. I'll just – I'll have both of them. I can have my cake and eat it too. Well, parents can't do that.'

B

In this and other ways, polyamorous families face institutional vulnerability just as homosexual, single or transgender parents do. Since these harms stem from social hostility, not polyamory itself, we redress these harms using education and legal activism rather than by preventing people from being polyamorous.

The other problems described by Sheff include the attachment of a child to people who leave the home, household crowding, tension caused by ex-partners, romantic conflicts and sibling jealousy. Sheff cites a child in a polyamorous family who acknowledges: 'There is jealousy, I guess, between my brother and sister and I. Because we have different dads, you know, there has always been that tension.'

A

A The Kardashian-Jenners. With divorce, remarriage and single parenting now common, and modelled even by A-list celebrities, family structures vary dramatically.

B A schedule of household chores in a plural family containing 41 children. Any large family is vulnerable to problems of organization and scarcity of resources. But these issues are problems of degree, not of kind, and are often surmountable.

Sunday Meal Schedule - 2008

	Mother On Duty	Breakfast Dishes Help	Dinner Help	Kids Breakfast
January 6	Carol	Sally	Sophia	Mary
January 13	Joyce	Aseneth	Sally	Sophia
January 20	Marie/Michelle	Dorothy	Aseneth	Sally
January 27	Susan	Guinevere/Elizabeth	Dorothy	Aseneth
February 3	Jestikah	Sharon	Guinevere/Elizabeth	Dorothy
February 10	Heather	Rebecca	Sharon	Guinevere/Elizabeth
February 17	Carol	Mary	Rebecca	Sharon
February 24	Joyce	Sophia	Mary	Rebecca
March 2	Marie/Michelle	Sally	Sophia	Mary
March 9	Susan	Aseneth	Sally	Sophia
March 16	Jestikah	Dorothy	Aseneth	Sally
March 23	Heather	Guinevere/Elizabeth	Dorothy	Aseneth
March 30	Carol	Sharon	Guinevere/Elizabeth	Dorothy
April 6	Joyce	Rebecca	Sharon	Guinevere/Elizabeth
April 13	Marie/Michelle	Mary	Rebecca	Sharon
April 20	Susan	Sophia	Mary	Rebecca
April 27	Jestikah	Sally	Sophia	Mary
May 4	Heather	Aseneth	Sally	Sophia
May 11	Carol	Dorothy	Aseneth	Sally
May 18	Joyce	Guinevere/Elizabeth	Dorothy	Aseneth
May 25	Marie/Michelle	Sharon	Guinevere/Elizabeth	Dorothy
June 1	Susan	Rebecca	Sharon	Guinevere/Elizabeth
June 8	Jestikah	Mary	Rebecca	Sharon
June 15	Heather	Sophia	Mary	Rebecca
June 22	Carol	Sally	Sophia	Mary
June 29	Joyce	Aseneth	Sally	Sophia
July 6	Marie/Michelle	Dorothy	Aseneth	Sally
July 13	Susan	Guinevere/Elizabeth	Dorothy	Aseneth
July 20	Jestikah	Sharon	Guinevere/Elizabeth	Dorothy
July 27	Heather	Rebecca	Sharon	Guinevere/Elizabeth

Dishwasher Checklist

B

None of these issues are unique to polyamory. They often arise in modern monogamous families, too, especially if the family is large, if a parent is previously divorced, has children from other relationships or is newly dating. From Henry VIII in sixteenth-century England to the Kardashians of modern America, complex family structures and ensuing strains are common in monogamous, as well as polyamorous life. If these facts do not challenge the permissibility of monogamy, why should they challenge the permissibility of nonmonogamy? More positively, the benefits of polyamorous life mirror those of blended monogamous families, where childcare is shared and children benefit from multiple role models.

Even if polyamorous families are akin to many modern monogamous families, we might think polyamorous relationships are troubled in other ways; that polyamory impedes love; that it is not special; that it is greedy; that it is too vulnerable, or not vulnerable enough.

A

B

Exclusive love for one person means you do not love anyone else. People typically have romantic love in mind when speaking of exclusivity, as many people also love their families and friends alongside their romantic partner.

A Shows like *Love Island* help illustrate that sexual desire and attraction are unpredictable. People can desire several people at once, and their desires can change dramatically.
B *Love Island* is famed for its love triangles. To be consistent, people who think polyamorists cannot love several people at once would also have to deny love triangles exist.
C Social norms of romantic life, adultery and divorce have changed to the point that they are even reflected in the lives of our presidents and future monarchs.

This does not seem right. Not only would we have to explain why so many polyamorous people misunderstand their own experiences, we would also have to deny the existence of love triangles, or messy affairs. *Le Mort d'Arthur, Gone with the Wind, Wuthering Heights, The Great Gatsby* and *Bridget Jones's Diary*: some of our greatest literature features passionate love triangles, and they are arguably so appealing as we know the emotion to be genuine.
That said, perhaps polyamorous love is shallow. Psychotherapist Robert Masters worries that having more than one lover allows underlying relationship issues to be ignored, and therefore precludes the formation of deeper attachments that come from working through problems.

This behaviour is bad, but not unique to romantic life, let alone polyamory. We could flit between friends to avoid confronting a disagreement, but this possibility is no reason to avoid having friends. Masters's view would also appear to have the implausible consequence that it is better to have one friend than many, to avoid impeding deep attachments. But since we can be deeply attached to close friends and family, it is not hard to imagine this happening in romantic life.

Some people think only exclusive love is special.

The problem with this idea is that 'specialness' is not the same as exclusivity. A parent can have a unique and special relationship with both of their two children. Neither relationship is undermined by the existence of the other. Similarly, romantic lovers share history, a specific language and a companionship that is not compromised by other relationships. If it were, then serial monogamy would also be problematic. Moreover, to have an exclusive relationship is also not to choose someone 'over everyone else'. We very rarely make explicit romantic choices between multiple suitors, let alone everyone else. Finally, the fact that special relationships are valuable actually motivates nonmonogamy, because nonmonogamous people want to increase the *amount* of this value they, and their partners, can experience.

c

This last point belies another worry: would widespread polyamory make it hard for people to find romantic partners? Would some people have many partners, and others none? For some, like 'incels' – the 'involuntary celibates' who think feminism stops them having romantic lives – this worry rests on the idea that people have a 'right' to a romantic partner. This view should be rejected. If we have a right to something, someone else has a duty to provide, or not prevent our access to it. Since romantic life is so personal, nobody has a duty to be our romantic partner, so there is no 'right' to a romantic partner.

The worry that polyamory would make it harder for some people to find love and intimacy is plausible only if polyamory meant that people formed exclusive gender-imbalanced romantic groups. But not all polyamorous relationships are heteronormative, and polyamory is more likely to facilitate *overlapping* non-exclusive relationship groups. Moreover, since polyamorous people reject the ideal of 'the one' romantic partner, people who make poor *monogamous* romantic companions, are more likely to have a flourishing romantic life.

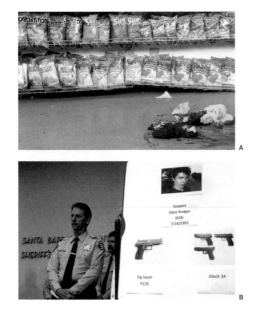

A

B

Incel is a recent term meaning 'involuntary celibate'. Incels are a predominantly male online sub-culture who espouse a range of misogynistic and antifeminist views about women, and the attitudes of women towards men. Their ideology has been linked to violence against women, including several mass shootings.

Aromantic people are not romantically drawn to other people and do not pursue romantic relationships. Some aromantics experience sexual attraction and have an active sex life, others do not.

A   Bloodied towels in a supermarket, following the attack of Incel Elliot Rodger (1991–2014).
B   A police display of Elliot Rodger and the weapons he used. The worry that nonmonogamy is a threat to successful monogamous dating says more about the perilous contemporary state of the latter, than the nascent state of the former.
C   Many societies over-privilege romantic relationships to the expense of other important relationships in life, like friendships.

C

Other critics of polyamory worry that it requires, or generates, greed. In discussing polyamory, Regnerus suggests that 'people "need" multiple partners like they need four houses or six automobiles', his implication being that having multiple partners is excessive. Perhaps this connection of polyamory with hedonism and greed stems from associations with the harems of historic Eastern cultures. Not only would this caricaturize modern polyamory, it echoes Westerners' pernicious orientalizing of different relationships models.

Besides, this way of thinking presupposes monogamous ideals by assuming that only one partner is appropriate. Similarly, if the greed critique applies to romantic life, we should expect it to apply to friendship, too. But someone with three friends is not greedier than someone with two. Moreover, nobody actually *needs* a romantic partner. Even if we need love or care, they can take platonic forms. Many people flourish while content with friends and family, and aromantic people never desire amorous relationships. While not aromantic, author Dolly Alderton has been vocal about the importance of female friendships, declaring them to be the greatest love story of her life, rather than any romantic pairing. Finally, isn't greed the unwillingness to share, i.e. the very attitude that polyamorous people contest by holding that love need not be exclusive?

Some might concede that polyamorous love is possible, only to worry that it will stifle romance. Will all the explicit listening, talking and boundaries prevent spontaneity, flirtation and seduction? A full answer depends partly on what we find romantic, but it is arguable that clear boundaries and communication help romance thrive. When we know someone's desires, aversions and expectations we can seduce with affection and respect. Ambiguity over boundaries and desires causes anxiety because people are unsure of how they are being treated, and it can help powerful people be disingenuous or manipulative.

We could accept this last thought only to raise a final concern: does polyamory expose us to *too much* excitement and vulnerability? Does polyamory carry an increased risk of loss?

The depiction of polyamory as resulting in tragedy and heartbreak is a common trope in popular culture – from films *Jules et Jim* (1962) to *The Dreamers* (2004) – which may have increased our perception of it as emotionally risky. Obviously, the more relationships we have, the greater the chances of heartbreak. Yet this is true both of a serial monogamist who has several relationships over time and someone with several concurrent relationships.

A

A. Break-up and loss are now a ubiquitous, but underappreciated, aspect of romantic life. Serial monogamy, in particular, encourages people to downplay the impact of successive traumatic break-ups, as these cheerful break-up cupcakes demonstrate.

B. Of all the tumultuous emotions, jealousy tends to attract the most attention, hence this stock image becoming an internationally appreciated meme. But even emotions that feel good, such as excitement, can be hard to handle or destabilize a relationship.

B

Arguably, however, polyamorous people are better placed to navigate heartbreak in comparison to monogamous people. If we subscribe to the monogamy ideal of 'the one', then the loss of a partner ramifies widely, because of their centrality to our lives and sense of self. If we reject this ideal, the loss of one partner, although devastating in its particularity, will have a restricted impact. Other partners can support us, and we are more likely to retain the confidence and self-esteem that often blooms in romantic relationships.

Another key concern with nonmonogamy is that jealousy over our partners' intimacy with other people cannot be tamed. Some people think this jealousy is justified, and so monogamy is a sensible way to avoid painful feelings.

To be jealous is to be pained by the worry that a rival threatens the affection we get from someone we care about, and to which we feel entitled. The role of the rival distinguishes jealousy from situations where we just fear that affections will wane. The role of entitlement differentiates jealousy from envy since when jealous, we feel that someone hovers to take what is 'rightly ours'.

A

A   A Voodoo practitioner prays to Erzulie Dantor, the goddess of jealousy, passion, romance, love and sex.
B   The coffin of María José Alvarado (1995–2014), who was killed, along with her sister, by her sister's jealous boyfriend. Defenders of jealousy often downplay its association with other toxic beliefs, such as patriarchal entitlement to women.

Jealousy may seem useful. Although it is painful, some people believe that jealousy helps us realize we care about someone, or that they care about us. It is a common trope in literature and film for a protagonist to discover they love someone only when a rival invokes their jealousy. Jealousy can therefore seem to prevent romantic complacency and indifference.

Even if jealousy helps some people in these ways, is that enough of a reason for jealousy to be defended, even promoted, as a character trait? There are good reasons to think not. For each useful instance of jealousy, there are many that are painfully volatile. Jealousy can spark anger and blame. Jealousy also seems connected closely to aggression, from the murderous rage of Shakespeare's Othello to ugly rows and social media disputes. These concerns are sufficient to undermine the idea that jealousy is valuable as a character trait.

B

A critic might reply that although jealousy can be disruptive, it reflects what we are owed in romantic life. The idea of entitlement in relationships is a murky one, but even if jealousy rests on some inchoate sense that we are not getting the affection we deserve, there may still be good moral or prudential reasons not to feel jealous. We think this about other emotions. For example, it can be useful to not feel terror in terrifying situations, as this helps us stay composed; or we may believe it is morally problematic to feel schadenfreude, even in response to the downfall of someone bad, because of what it implies about our character. Analogously, even if jealousy tracks a lack of affection, feeling it is unhelpful and perhaps in tension with having a kind, loving character.

Many nonmonogamous people want to tame jealousy in order to prevent it from interfering with their ability to love other people. This desire is not simply defensive, because many nonmonogamous people want to be able to feel joy when their partners are intimate with others. Arguably, everyone would benefit from the ability to feel good about the flourishing pleasures of people they care about, especially in situations that are often fraught with competition or anxiety.

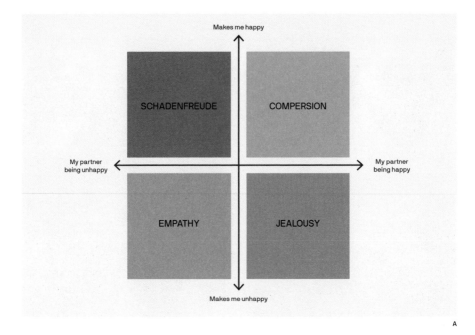

Makes me happy

SCHADENFREUDE

COMPERSION

My partner being unhappy ← → My partner being happy

EMPATHY

JEALOUSY

Makes me unhappy

A

A Compersion is often called the 'opposite' of jealousy, but since relationships between emotions are quite complex, as hinted at in this diagram, we should resist thinking that jealousy has one opposite.

B People might be able to make progress in resisting jealousy and associated behaviours without being able to appreciate the good experiences in the lives of others, and vice versa.

Within the polyamorous community, this positive emotion towards a partner's intimacy with other people has been called 'compersion'. The term supposedly originated in a San Franciscan commune, and has been defined in different ways. In their polyamorous relationship manual *More Than Two* (2014), Franklin Veaux and Eve Rickert describe compersion as 'a feeling of joy experienced when a partner takes pleasure from another romantic or sexual relationship'. In another book, *Opening Up* (2008), Tristan Taormino cites someone who calls compersion 'acceptance of, and vicarious enjoyment for, a lover's joy'. Compersion is occasionally seen as the opposite of jealousy, but some may worry that compersion looks more like pride, or masochistic pleasure.

In fact, compersion is best understood as a response to the intimate flourishing of other people. If we are compersive, we feel good because our partner's life is enriched by someone else. We must *feel* positive not just *believe* that our partner is flourishing, and we must view their intimacy as actually pleasing. This is why compersion is not like masochistic pleasure, where our unpleasant feelings are disconnected from our positive evaluation of a situation.

Similarly, when we are compersive, we feel good about intimacy that the people concerned think is good. Therefore compersion, unlike pride, requires us to be empathetic and understand how other people think and feel. Finally, compersion is not vicarious enjoyment because we can be compersive without wanting what our partner has.

This may sound good in theory, but hard to obtain in practice. How can we become compersive and replace jealousy with feelings of joy?

There are two steps to this process: to address our jealous tendencies, and to focus on the flourishing of other people. To address jealousy, we need to know why it arises. In discussion of jealousy, two features are often mentioned: entitlement and vulnerability. Some theorists think one feature predominates, but we make better sense of most jealousy if we believe both are involved. This is because we can understand why jealousy sometimes resembles indignation, and why attempts to address entitlement are rarely sufficient to tame it.

Compersion is often described as jealousy's opposite, and is the feeling of joy towards a partner's intimacy experienced with other people. The term has become widespread in nonmonogamous communities to describe positive emotions arising from nonexclusive intimacy.

B

We are vulnerable because humans are social creatures who depend on and become attached to other people. Other people care for us, make us feel secure, help us explore ourselves and our environment and contribute to our sense of identity. Thus we are hurt, and our identity is destabilized, when people leave or their affections wane. This vulnerability is especially acute in romantic relationships that are contingently formed and based on an evaluation of our desirability. Awareness of this vulnerability might make us anxious.

We can manage our dependence on others by balancing our ability to be intimate with personal resilience. But this balance is often elusive. Stress, change, trauma or an insecure personality can make us possessive, that is, overly reliant on the presence of other people. In most societies, these possessive behaviours are justified by social norms and ideals of entitlement that portray possessiveness as an ordinary or warranted part of romantic life. Indeed, obsessive or jealous behaviour is often portrayed as the height of romance in popular culture. From Ross's jealousy in *Friends* (1994–2004), to Edward's controlling behaviour in *Twilight* (2005) we are told that these traits are the ultimate portrayal of love, when in fact they are deeply unhealthy and, in extreme cases, abusive. These ideals intersect with monogamous ideals. People not only expect extensive attention from a romantic partner, but also expect that attention to be exclusive.

A

B

C

A   People protest the film
    50 Shades of Grey (2015),
    concerned that its unnuanced
    portrayal of 'domination' and
    'submission' romanticizes
    abusive behaviour.
B   Mixed martial arts fighter
    Jason Miller is arrested
    on charges of stalking
    and domestic abuse.
C   It can often be hard to
    notice, at first glance, the
    extent to which romantic
    tropes rest on broader social
    norms about gender and
    power relations that many
    would now reject.

Vulnerability prompts possessive behaviours, which are subsequently cast as reasonable in the light of social norms of entitlement. Any attempt to tackle jealousy must therefore address entitlement and personal vulnerability. Since personal vulnerabilities are often resistant to direct reasoning, especially when they are anchored in childhood experiences, merely trying to change our beliefs about what to expect from a romantic partner may not be sufficient to reduce our jealousy. In practice, however, our efforts to confront our entitlement and to manage our vulnerability will be interconnected.

We gain a critical understanding of entitlement by considering our society's romantic norms and ideals. What is the predominant conception of romantic commitment? How do people think about exclusivity? Do we personally endorse these ideals? Such general reflections intersect with personal consideration of our romantic expectations and boundaries. What do we want from our partner, and why do we want these things? What triggers our fears and anxieties? What kinds of affirmation do we need?

A

Emotional management can be achieved in a variety of ways, from reconsidering the beliefs underlying our feelings (e.g. overcoming the belief that flying is dangerous may reduce feelings of anxiety on flights) through to indirect attempts to reframe how we are feeling (e.g. breathing exercises or listening to calming music).

Self-help books for nonmonogamous people often give advice about how to manage vulnerability through indirect forms of emotional management, perhaps by slowly exposing ourselves to situations that previously would have elicited jealousy, for example, or through more extensive communication with a partner. Since uncertainty often amplifies anxiety, voicing jealousy can weaken its grip. Similarly, we can do much to cultivate a supportive environment. We can see a therapist, talk to friends or set aside time to check in with our partner and voice concerns without judgment. When accompanied by efforts to show love and affirmation, and to simply make time to listen to a partner, these practices can help us contextualize, understand and reduce our jealousy.

Minimizing jealousy sets us on the way towards feeling compersive. But compersion requires us to actively acknowledge and appreciate how other people are flourishing.

To do this, we have to redirect our attention and exercise our imagination. We need to try to view experiences from the perspective of our partner and the other people who care for them. Instead of focusing on what we lack, we can concentrate on what a partner gains when they are with another. We must also interrogate any habit of automatically thinking of others as rivals. Occasionally people *are* rivals – they want to hurt us or disregard our interests – but this is rare. The 'rival' is such a culturally dominant notion because portrayals of romance rarely make space for non-exclusive forms of care and affection, so we might have to generate our own examples or join nonmonogamous communities. Often another person looms large as a rival because we know little about them. Once we understand more of someone's personality, history and interests – an effort that requires empathy – it is harder to dismiss them as threatening.

Compersion is something to aim for.

A   This text conversation shows what compersion might look like in practice. Good communication helps people understand both their emotions and their meta-emotions, that is, their feelings about their feelings.

B   Much hostility to unfamiliar forms of life stems from failures of imagination. As larger audiences begin to engage with artistic representations of non-normative relationships, in literature, film and television, this imaginational deficit will be less severe.

But since the road from jealousy to compersion is complex, and social contexts are often hostile, we should be wary of demanding compersion of others, or castigating ourselves for not feeling it. Like other kinds of anxiety, such as fear of flying, jealousy can be out of step with our beliefs. In those situations, however, the move from accepting jealousy to seeing it as problematic is positive. Anything beyond that, such as feeling compersion, is a bonus.

Polyamorous relationships, and by extension many other nonmonogamous relationships, can be loving, special and romantic, and can equip people with norms and ideals that help them navigate vulnerability, loss, jealousy and raising a family.

A   The many wives of the chief of Oudjilla, Cameroon, perform a traditional dance. As we have stressed earlier in this book, plural marriage is not a unitary phenomenon. In this respect, plural marriage resembles monogamous marriage, or friendship; institutions which have varied greatly over time and between societies.

B   The marriage of South African president Jacob Zuma (b. 1942) to his third wife in 2010. Modern critiques of plural marriage must avoid the racism, sexism and colonial assumptions that previous critiques were based upon.

C   A woman weeps following the removal of over 400 children from her polygamous Mormon community in 2008 for the children's safety. To discuss or defend a form of life is not to endorse or downplay bad instances of that form of life. Like any kind of marriage, specific plural marriages can be damaging and abusive, or reinforce existing social harms.

c

Recognition of these facts leads some to suggest that plural marriages should be permitted, either as an extension of existing marriage institutions or as a feature of minimal marriages. To many, however, plural marriage is a step too far.

Thom Brooks's arguments against polygamy are representative. In his article 'The Problem with Polygamy' (2009), Brooks argues that polygamy is harmful and inegalitarian. He offers distressing evidence, from the USA and countries in Africa, the Middle East and Asia, that some polygamous marriages harm women by lowering their self-esteem, reducing their marital satisfaction, making them vulnerable to post-natal depression, increasing the likelihood they will be abused and raising their risk of contracting STIs.

In reviewing the literature about the impact of polygamy on families Salman Elbedour and colleagues argue that polygamous families are a 'fertile breeding ground for behaviour problems in children' because of four risk factors: marital conflict, marital distress, absent fathers and financial stress.

A   B

In a family with one husband and several wives and children, marital conflicts are harmful because children may, unwittingly or otherwise, be encouraged to take sides, find themselves the target of a parent's displaced marital frustration or become aggressive themselves in reflection of parental conflict. Polygynous marriages are also associated with jealousy and anxiety, which are inherently stressful and undermine the mental health of a parent, which may in turn diminish their ability to care for a child. Polygynous families may be prone to disintegration, caused by the addition of new wives and the subsequent absence of the father. Children grieve absent fathers, and they are also harmed by reduced parental care or lack of role models. Finally, polygynous families typically include more children than monogamous families, which makes them prone to financial strain, especially as women in polygynous households are less likely to work outside of the home. Financial distress is connected to personal tension, and family poverty is linked to a range of negative outcomes for children, from educational achievement to overall health.

Polygynandry is a marriage or relationship between multiple men and multiple women, as opposed to one man and several women, or one woman and several men.

It is hard to say, however, whether these problems stem from plural marriage *as such,* from the fact that such marriages are heavily stigmatized, from the fact that such marriages attract certain kinds of people or from the fact that such marriages are permitted or prevalent in misogynistic and patriarchal societies.

The critical focus on polygamy often centres on religious communities where there is commonly little or no egalitarian ethos and men dominate. Similarly, critics of polygamy typically focus on polygyny and overlook other kinds of plural marriage such as polyandry or polygynandry (marriages between multiple men and multiple women). This approach is heteronormative in overlooking lesbians and gays who want group marriages.

Polygamy is a varied institution, and so must be evaluated in its specific cultural contexts. Even if some plural marriages are harmful, others may not be. Elbedour and colleagues note that their conclusion – that polygamy is harmful for children – 'has not been borne out consistently in the extant literature'.

C

To take one example, in a careful study of 56 diverse villages in Tanzania, David Lawson and colleagues found that studies that sought to aggregate data from across a country, in order to gauge whether polygyny is problematic, paint a misleading picture of polygyny in its particularity. Apparently negative correlations between the prevalence of polygyny and poor food security and poor child health neglect important differences between individual communities. Ecological features, such as differences in climate, or social factors, such as access to education, were to blame for poor health of polygynous children in specific communities, but not in others. They conclude that being a polygynous household is not itself an indicator of poor child health and well-being since 'polygyny is also a diverse institution with considerable cultural variation'.

More broadly, shouldn't people be as free to enter a harmful plural marriage as they are to enter a harmful monogamous marriage? Many assume that as long as people give consent they can marry whom they like, irrespective of whether their marriage will be imperfect, restrictive or harmful. If the state does not prevent monogamous people from marrying badly, it should not prevent nonmonogamous people from marrying badly either.

A **'hub' partner,** in a typical polygynous or polyandrous marriage, is the male or female partner to whom the other people are married, where those other people are not married to each other.

Polyfidelity is when the people in a nonmonogamous relationship agree to be romantically and/or sexually faithful to each other alone, and have no additional partners.

A/B Two alternative models for plural marriage. Since plural marriage is seldom taken seriously, little thought has gone into how the institution might be designed. Legitimate concerns about power of entry and exit to the marriage, the distribution of rights and duties within the marriage and the place of children within a family, might be surmountable in principle.

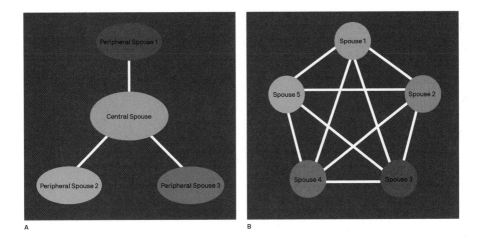

A   B

Brooks's main criticism, however, is that inequality is a *structural* feature of polygamy, because the central 'hub' partner has greater control over the ability of others to join and leave the marriage.

This concern applies to any plural marriage where one hub partner, man or woman, has greater power. But several answers are readily available.

Most notably, plural marriages can be structured in different ways, of which the hub-and-spoke model is only one. Gregg Strauss, in his article 'Is Polygamy Inherently Unequal?' (2012), argues convincingly that two alternative models can avoid the issues associated with unequal power over entry to the marriage and divorce. In the first alternative model, 'polyfidelity', everyone in the marriage is married to everyone else, rather than one 'hub' being married to multiple 'spokes'. In the second model, 'molecular' polygamy, each spouse within a marriage can marry more partners as they please. So, even if strict marital equality is as important as Brooks and others believe, governments could permit plural marriages as long as they take one of these two forms.

A

But is strict equality important, and is it something the state should be concerned with? We might think that some degree of inequality, of power, resources, time and so on, will arise in any marriage, at least for periods of time, if not for its entirety. Moreover, since personal relationships are shaped by broader social norms, inequality in romantic life is likely to be the result of social inequality. For example, if economically lower-class women are viewed as socially inferior to middle-class men, a monogamous relationship between those people in that society might reproduce unequal power dynamics. But we address inequality by addressing those harmful sexist and classist norms, not by banning monogamy.

Ronald Den Otter argues that plural marriages have social value as 'experiments in living'. If allowed, people could explore uncommon lifestyles. Without such experimentation we cannot know which intimate arrangements best help people to live flourishing lives, especially as our society changes with the second demographic transition.

B

A   These women are from four generations of under-age marriage. The monogamy ideal does not prevent marriages from being exploitive or unequal in practice.

B   This female refugee is about to marry an older man. In many countries, women and girls lack the socio-economic and political power to contract marriages as equal parties.

The best way to find out which kinds of relationship will work is to encourage people to experiment without fear of state sanction.

Many of the terms and practices contemporary nonmonogamous people take for granted arose in these experimental scenarios, such as in the Kerista commune in San Francisco (1950s to 1990s), the American neo-pagan Church of All Worlds (1960s to present day) or the ZEGG (Centre for Experimental Cultural and Social Design) community in Germany (1990s to present day). The ZEGG community, for example, aims to encourage a balance between individual parental care and community care, with children of the community learning and playing together in a communal space.

We do not need to adopt a carefree attitude to harm and inequality in order to think that plural marriage should be permissible. Instead, we simply need to recognize that plural marriages, like monogamous marriages, are not inherently harmful and do not necessarily compromise free will or autonomy.

In multicultural societies where polygamy is not legal, such as the USA or the UK, attitudes towards nonmonogamy correlate strongly with racial, financial and educational privilege. Sociologists Elisabeth Sheff and Corie Hammers found this in their study of polyamorous and kink communities. In aggregating the findings of 36 different studies, they found that the communities 'were overwhelmingly white, with relatively high socio-economic status.' Some potential reasons for this are that nonmonogamous communities rely on the internet which reinforces existing forms of social privilege, and that existing privileges can mitigate some of the possible negative outcomes of nonmonogamy, including discrimination, harmful tokenism and the cost of adopting an additional problematic social identity.

A

Sheff and Hammers also note that many nonmonogamous people have social privilege and a good education but a low income. This suggests that the pursuit of nonmonogamy may reflect political ideologies more than wealth, with liberals being more open to nonmonogamy than conservatives.

A   Protesters against same-sex marriage in Maryland, USA, in 2012. Historically, defenders of 'traditional' marriage have also opposed mixed-race marriages and marriage between people of different religions, and were often offended by any proposed changes to marriage law.

B   LGBT and polyamorous pride activism and marches, like this one in Canada, illustrate the importance of social recognition for marginalized groups. Over time, recognition also changes wider attitudes.

As Nathan Rambukkana notes in his book *Fraught Intimacies* (2015), in emphasizing consent and honesty, nonmonogamous people can be blind to differences of power, privilege and vulnerability. Nonmonogamous discourse must be careful to avoid presupposing everyone is a confident individual, clear in their thoughts, desires and feelings. Many people are uncertain or ambivalent, or are better able to understand themselves and make decisions in conversation with other people. Nonmonogamous communities need to accommodate such differences of personality.

B

A

Similarly, in focusing on how people communicate in a situation (clearly, honestly), we can neglect important differences in power and privilege. It is one thing to be a rich, middle-aged, white, male Californian who wants to have an open relationship, and quite another to be a queer Mexican woman in a polyamorous triad, or a young, poor Bedouin Arab woman in a polygamous marriage. Nonmonogamous practices must accommodate the fact that not everyone is equally placed to express themselves with the same ease, free of consequences. This is especially important because most societies are still sexist and oppressive, and men have disproportionate power and influence. Nonmonogamous relationships, particularly if driven underground in a hostile society, risk reproducing these negative dynamics, especially if the people involved are unable or unwilling to re-evaluate their privilege and entitlement.

Finally, nonmonogamous people can be seduced by unrealistic ideals. Formed as a response to the monogamous romantic ideal of 'the one', the single source of emotional and sexual intimacy, nonmonogamous people may yearn for 'the many', a life with several harmoniously loving partners where communication is effortless and compersion abounds. Just as monogamous ideals can overlook how people experience desire, attraction and the need for multiple kinds of relationship in life, polyamorous ideals might overlook the ways that people can be radically different, introverted, value their own space or struggle with jealousy.

All relationships benefit from realism.

A In countries like Chad, where polygamy is common, the framework of liberal individualism, with emphasis on choice and equality, is as alien as polygamy is to many liberals.

B A 'throuple' talk about their relationship on the television show *Good Morning Britain*. Attempts to secure recognition for non-normative lifestyles often involve the strategic emphasis of similarities to normative relationships.

B

A

Monogamy works for some, but not others.

As Terri Conley's study shows, many people feel that monogamy best fosters commitment, trust, meaningfulness and passionate intimacy. Most people also frown upon nonmonogamy, associating it with instability and jealousy.

The positive evaluation of monogamy has survived shifts in its nature as an ideal. Nowadays, many people happily pursue serial monogamy, having one partner at a time without expecting to have one partner for life. Longer life expectancies mean that there is room for several long marriages in one lifetime, and modern technology makes it easier to find new partners.

Yet we have also seen that monogamy, let alone monogamous marriage, is not the only context in which we can nurture romantic love, sexual fulfilment or family. Some people find monogamy restrictive, or at odds with their experience of love and desire. We have seen that monogamy is not 'natural' in any unambiguous sense, but has proved, instead, to be an alluring social ideal.

But this ideal is under threat. As the sexual revolution proceeds into the information age, and egalitarian norms of romantic life take hold, monogamy's practical demands are increasingly unclear. For some, sexual fidelity is paramount; for others, love and emotional intimacy take priority. Some prize domesticity; others emphasize shared values and projects, or quality time spent together. These disagreements help us see monogamy as one form of life among others, and that the distinction between monogamous and nonmonogamous relationships is rarely absolute.

As with any marginalized or non-normative form of life, we can learn much from nonmonogamy, even if we continue to personally favour monogamous relationships. It is easier to foster tolerance, and consider alternative romantic possibilities, when we recognize existing diversity in romantic life and the power of social norms.

A Societies can change faster than the ideals that circulate within them. The social world of the 1950s is gone, but the powerful vision of a small, romantically exclusive family remains.

B Alternatives to heteronormative life are increasingly visible, both in everyday life and in our media. The long-term effects of these revolutions in romantic life and marriage law remain to be seen.

B

This diversity provides the backdrop to any romantic choice. Although most monogamous relationships are consented to, this consent could be anchored in an understanding of available alternatives, what monogamy involves and what monogamy restricts.

This understanding is vital as monogamy is increasingly pursued on dating apps. While these apps offer an expanded choice of partners and a route to alternative relationships, they can also produce feelings of uncertainty, anxiety and reduced self-worth. A greater awareness of our options will make contextualizing or opting-out of these romantic practices easier. Moreover, It can be easy to overlook the benefits that monogamy forecloses. As well as having value in themselves, love, care, sexuality and romantic relationships have instrumental value. The more relationships we have, the more secure and resilient we become. Other people direct us towards new interests, values and self-knowledge, hold us accountable, burst inflated egos and supply us with emotional and practical resources. While true of friendship or serial monogamy, these benefits accrue with greater intimacy and intensity in nonmonogamous life.

Monogamy limits the number of romantically loving relationships we may have at once to one. But that fact also shapes the *kind* of relationship we desire.

A

A	A couple kiss on a swingers' cruise. Such 'casual' encounters can be conducted with as much care and respect for someone's desires and boundaries as the best monogamous courtship.
B	A polygamist family of one father, three mothers and 21 children in Salt Lake Valley, USA. Neither monogamy or nonmonogamy starts from a position of theoretical advantage. A full investigation of both must attend to their harms and benefits, and the traits required to practise them well.

B

If we can only have one romantic relationship, we will want our partner to be sufficiently good overall, rather than exceptional in a few respects. Monogamy also typically limits our ability to notice, appreciate and respond to many romantic and sexual experiences. Whether we resist attraction and desire, or strive to not feel it in the first place, we reshape how alive we are to these valuable things. Ideally, people would choose to be monogamous fully aware of what they lose out on.

Attention to nonmonogamous norms and practices can also alter our understanding of commitment. Nonmonogamous people typically do not view commitment as something established through becoming exclusive and then defended from violations. Commitment is instead an active process, shown in action constantly.

Nonmonogamous people also value good communication as a means of defusing anxiety, removing uncertainty and processing jealousy. Good communication requires practice and demands tolerance in the face of inevitable mistakes and defensiveness. Everyone can benefit from better communicative practices in romantic life, not only for the practical benefits, but also because they manifest love and respect.

A

Finally, compersion, joyful feelings towards the intimate flourishing of those we love, is more likely when we accept contingency and regard commitment as an active process. Compersion is sometimes fragile, since jealousy is hard to uproot, but it can be contagious and transformative.

Does monogamy have a bright future?

The second demographic transition has developed unevenly, so monogamy will be a major presence in the short term because some societies have yet to experience the broader social changes associated with longer life expectancies, rising divorce, cohabitation and the sexual revolution. Alternatives to monogamy will become more visible, however, as societies change. Polyamorous ideals, in particular, resonate with the growing desire for romantic relationships to be based on emotional intimacy, and personality, not social status.

Romantic anarchy may also have impact as people realize that there are many different personal relationships, and that ethical distinctions between them marginalize alternative kinds of flourishing. Similarly, the institution of monogamous marriage may come to seem inflexible as functionally similar relationships remain unprotected. Instead, people may be eager to safeguard love, care and tenderness wherever they are found, whether that is in a monogamous relationship, close friendship, parental relationship or nonmonogamous network.

Love's future will be as diverse as love's past. Monogamy will not disappear, but nonmonogamous alternatives will seem increasingly normal, and multi-partner relationships may receive social recognition. As they do, everyone will be better able to cultivate meaningful relationships because it will be easier to ask: Which kind of romantic life, if any, is right for me and those I love?

B

Further Reading

Barker, Meg John, *Rewriting the Rules: An Anti Self-Help Guide to Love, Sex and Relationships* (Abingdon; New York, NY: Routledge, 2012)

Betzig, Laura L., *Despotism and Differential Reproduction: A Darwinian View of History* (New York, NY: Aldine Publishing Co., 1986)

Bogaert, Anthony F., *Understanding Asexuality* (Lanham, MD: Rowman & Littlefield, 2012)

Brake, Elizabeth, ed., *After Marriage: Rethinking Marital Relationships* (New York, NY: Oxford University Press, 2016)

Brake, Elizabeth, *Minimizing Marriage: Marriage, Morality, and the Law* (Oxford: Oxford University Press, 2012)

Brooks, Thom, 'The Problem with Polygamy', *Philosophical Topics*, 37, 2 (2009), 109–22

Brunning, Luke, 'Compersion: An Alternative to Jealousy?', *Journal of the American Philosophical Association* (2020)

Brunning, Luke, 'The Distinctiveness of Polyamory', *Journal of Applied Philosophy*, 35, 3 (2018), 513–31

Chambers, Clare, *Against Marriage: An Egalitarian Defence of the Marriage-Free State* (Oxford: Oxford University Press, 2017)

Conley, Terri D. et al., 'The Fewer the Merrier?: Assessing Stigma Surrounding Consensually Non-Monogamous Romantic Relationships', *Analyses of Social Issues and Public Policy*, 13, 1 (2013), 1–30

Coontz, Stephanie, *Marriage, a History: How Love Conquered Marriage* (New York, NY; London: Penguin, 2005)

Dabhoiwala, Faramerz, *The Origins of Sex: A History of The First Sexual Revolution* (London: Penguin, 2012)

De Sousa, Ronald, *Love: A Very Short Introduction*, Vol. 415 (Oxford; New York, NY: Oxford University Press, 2015)

Den Otter, Ronald C., *In Defense of Plural Marriage* (New York, NY: Cambridge University Press, 2015)

Earp, Brian D. and Savulescu, Julian, *Love is the Drug: The Chemical Future of Our Relationships* (Manchester: Manchester University Press, 2020)

Emens, Elizabeth F., 'Monogamy's Law: Compulsory Monogamy and Polyamorous Existence', *NYU Review of Law and Social Change*, 29, 2 (2004), 277–376

Friedan, Betty, *The Feminine Mystique* (New York, NY: W.W. Norton & Company, 1963)

Giddens, Anthony, *The Transformation of Intimacy: Sexuality, Love and Eroticism in Modern Societies* (Cambridge: Polity, 1992)

Halwani, Raja, *Philosophy of Love, Sex, and Marriage: An Introduction* (London: Routledge, 2012)

Illouz, Eva, *Why Love Hurts: A Sociological Explanation* (Cambridge: Polity, 2012)

Jenkins, Carrie, *What Love Is: And What It Could Be* (New York, NY: Basic Books, 2017)

Kanazawa, Satoshi and Still, Mary C., 'Why Monogamy?', *Social Forces*, 78, 1 (1999), 25–50

Klesse, Christian, 'Polyamory: Intimate Practice, Identity or Sexual Orientation?', *Sexualities*, 17, 1–2 (2014), 81–99

Marcuse, Herbert, *Eros and Civilization: A Philosophical Inquiry Into Freud* (Boston: Beacon Press, 1974)

Marino, Patricia, *Philosophy of Sex and Love: An Opinionated Introduction* (New York, NY: Routledge, 2019)

May, Simon, *Love: A History* (New Haven, CT: Yale University Press, 2011)

McKeever, Natasha, 'Is the Requirement of Sexual Exclusivity Consistent with Romantic Love?', *Journal of Applied Philosophy*, 34, 3 (2017), 353–69

McMurtry, John, 'Monogamy: A Critique', *The Monist*, 56, 4 (1972), 587–99

Rambukkana, Nathan, *Fraught Intimacies: Non/Monogamy in the Public Sphere* (Vancouver; Toronto: University of British Columbia Press, 2015)

Regnerus, Mark, *Cheap Sex: The Transformation of Men, Marriage, and Monogamy* (New York, NY: Oxford University Press, 2017)

Scheidel, Walter, 'Sex and Empire' in Morris, Ian and Scheidel, Walter eds., *The Dynamics of Ancient Empires: State Power from Assyria to Byzantium* (New York, NY; Oxford: Oxford University Press, 2009), 255–324

Sheff, Elisabeth, and Hammers, Corie, 'The Privilege of Perversities: Race, Class and Education Among Polyamorists and Kinksters', *Psychology & Sexuality*, 2, 3 (2011), 198–223

Sheff, Elisabeth, *The Polyamorists Next Door: Inside Multiple-Partner Relationships and Families*, (Lanham, MD; Plymouth: Rowman & Littlefield, 2013)

Strauss, Gregg, 'Is Polygamy Inherently Unequal?', *Ethics*, 122, 3 (2012), 516–44

Taormino, Tristan, *Opening Up: A Guide to Creating and Sustaining Open Relationships* (Hoboken, NJ: Cleis Press, 2008)

Therborn, Göran, *Between Sex And Power: Family in the World 1900-2000* (London: Routledge, 2004)

Veaux, Franklin and Rickert, Eve, *More Than Two: A Practical Guide to Ethical Polyamory* (Portland, OR: Thorntree Press, 2014)

Witte, John, *The Western Case for Monogamy Over Polygamy* (New York, NY: Cambridge University Press, 2015)

Picture Credits

Every effort has been made to locate and credit copyright holders of the material reproduced in this book. The author and publisher apologize for any omissions or errors, which can be corrected in future editions.

a = above, b = below,
c = centre, l = left, r = right

Shutterstock
50r Jonathan Perugia/
Shutterstock
51 Popperfoto via Getty
Images/Getty Images
52 *The Saltonstall Family*,
1636, David des Granges
(1611–75), photo © Tate
53 © Victoria and Albert
Museum, London
54 Kirn Vintage Stock/
Corbis via Getty
Images
55a Fox Photos/Getty Images
55b Popperfoto via Getty
Images/Getty Images
56 H. Armstrong Roberts/
ClassicStock/
Getty Images
58l Bill Eppridge/The LIFE
Picture Collection
via Getty Images
58r John Dominis/The LIFE
Picture Collection
via Getty Images
59 © Burt Glinn/
Magnum Photos
60l Nicholas Bailey/
Shutterstock
60r Nicolas Maeterlinck/
EPA/Shutterstock
61 Sean Gallup/
Getty Images
62 Gallo Images/
Shutterstock
64a Olivier Chouchana/
Gamma-Rapho
via Getty Images
64b Eugene Hoshiko/AP/
Shutterstock
65 Veejay Villafranca/
Bloomberg
via Getty Images
66 Andrew Councill/AFP
via Getty Images
67 Katie Jones/Variety/
Shutterstock
68 Noorullah Shirzada/
AFP via Getty Images
69 Naver
70–1 © Gueorgui Pinkhassov/
Magnum Photos

72–3 © Martin Parr/
Magnum Photos
74 Media Whalestock
75 Sasha/Hulton Archive/
Getty Images
76 Lucas Schifres/
Getty Images
77 Joaquin Sarmiento/
AFP via Getty Images
78 Visual China Group
via Getty Images
80 Jack Taylor/Getty Images
81 Denise Truscello/
WireImage
82 Education Images/
Universal Images Group
via Getty Images
83l AVEN
83r fefedlove / Reddit.com
84 WENN Rights Ltd/
Alamy Stock Photo
85 Killing Kittens #WeAreKK
campaign. Photo by
Amelia Troubridge
86 Nikki Kahn/
The Washington Post
via Getty Images
88 OKCupid
89 Shawn Goldberg/
Shutterstock
93–5 Stephan Gladieu/
Getty Images
96 Reuters/Callaghan
O'Hare
97 Courtesy Melanie Pinola
98 Ray Tang/Shutterstock
99 Alain Jocard/AFP
via Getty Images
100 Kevin Mazur/Getty
Images for Yeezy
Season 3
101 Stephan Gladieu/
Getty Images
102 ITV/Shutterstock
103 Victoria Jones - WPA
Pool/Getty Images
104a Robyn Beck/AFP
via Getty Images
104b Michael Nelson/EPA/
Shutterstock
105 Vladimir Smirnov/TASS
via Getty Images

106 MissPixieParty /
Etsy.com
107 AntonioGuillem
108 Thony Belizaire/AFP
via Getty Images
109 Esteban Felix/AP/
Shutterstock
111 November.27
112l Leon Neal/AFP
via Getty Images
112r Mark Boster/*Los
Angeles Times*
via Getty Images
113 Ricky Swift/Icon
Sportswire via
Getty Images
115 Andy Cross/*The Denver
Post* via Getty Images
116a Eric Travers/Gamma-
Rapho via Getty Images
116b Foto24/Gallo Images/
Getty Images
117 Reuters/Jessica
Rinaldi
118 Stephan Gladieu/
Getty Images
119 José Nicolas/Corbis
via Getty Images
122–3 Allison Joyce/
Getty Images
124 Patrick Semansky/AP/
Shutterstock
125 Shawn Goldberg
126 Orhan Cicek/Anadolu
Agency/Getty Images
127 Ken McKay/ITV/
Shutterstock
128–9 © Gueorgui Pinkhassov/
Magnum Photos
130 © Jean Gaumy/
Magnum Photos
131 © Martin Parr/
Magnum Photos
132 Christinne Muschi/
Toronto Star via
Getty Images
133 Stephan Gladieu/
Getty Images
134 Artur Reszko/EPA-EFE/
Shutterstock
135 © Jonas Bendiksen/
Magnum Photos

Index

Acknowledgments:
This book owes its existence to many people.
I would like to thank Patricia Marino who
recommended me for this project, and Jane,
Izzy and Phoebe at Thames & Hudson for nurturing
it throughout. Although I wrote the text during
a precarious time, the support of my family and
friends has been unshakable. Together, you taught
me to think, and to love. I hope I have honored your
different points of view. Most of all, I am grateful
to Jenny for helping this book, and its author,
try to be the best versions of themselves.

First published in the United Kingdom in 2020
by Thames & Hudson Ltd, 181A High Holborn,
London WC1V 7QX

First published in the United States of America
in 2020 by Thames & Hudson Inc., 500 Fifth Avenue,
New York, New York 10110

Does Monogamy Work? © 2020
Thames & Hudson Ltd, London

Text © 2020 Luke Brunning
General Editor: Matthew Taylor

For image copyright information, see pp. 138–139

British Library Cataloguing-in-Publication Data
A catalogue record for this book is available from
the British Library

Library of Congress Control Number 2020931764

ISBN 978-0-500-29569-4

Printed and bound in Slovenia by DZS Grafik